DAWN AT MIDNIGHT

DAWN AT MIDNIGHT

A NOVEL

CHUCK CORWIN

Tercentenary Publication

2010

DAWN AT MIDNIGHT - A NOVEL – Published by the Rev. Dr. Ashish Amos of the Indian Society for Promoting Christian Knowledge (ISPCK), Post Box 1585, Kashmere Gate, Delhi-110006.

© Chuck Corwin, 2010

All rights reserved. No part of this book may be reproduced or transmitted in any form or by any means, electronic, mechanical, photocopying, recording, or by any information storage and retrieval system, without the prior permission in writing from the publisher.

The views expressed in the book are those of the author and the publisher takes no responsibility for any of the statements.

ISBN: 978-81-8465-087-7

Laser typeset by **ISPCK,** Post Box 1585, 1654, Madarsa Road, Kashmere Gate, Delhi-110006
Tel: 23866323/22
e-mail: ashish@ispck.org.in • ella@ispck.org.in
website: www.ispck.org.in

to grandchildren –

        EMILY
        ELEANOR
        PAUL
        SONJA
        MICHAEL
        MATHIAS
        CHARLES
        MELANIE
        CHAPMAN

The grace of God has dawned upon the world
bringing healing to all mankind.
Titus 2:11

"And then, into this tasteless heap of gold and marble,
He came, light... emphatically human, deliberately
provincial, Galilean, and at that moment gods
and nations cease to be and man came into being."
Boris Pasternak, ***Dr. Zhivago***

PREFACE

Twentieth-century ideologies took us to the depths of intellectual and moral depravity but the grace of God brought us out. I have pieced together episodes, including our own, of those returning to war-ravaged Europe, defeated Japan, and strife-riven China. Events follow the timeline of two interactive families—Kingsbury from the West and Nakajima from the East.

1

The moon, pale and yellow at first, mounted higher until its silver rays lit red-roofed stone houses nestled among the hills. Near a furrowed field outside the town stood a dilapidated barn covered with yellow-green moss. Bivouacked inside were eight medical corpsmen of the US 112th Sanitation Battalion. The open field sloped downward to the Meuthe river then upward to the town. On the right could be seen a small graveyard next to a church with two crucifixes jutting up from the earth, one of which leaned at a 30-degree angle and had the horizontal beam broken off, evidently struck by a stray shell. Private Matt

Kingsbury peered through a barn door ajar. "The town's dark. Not a flicker," he said out loud.

"Idiot! We're trying to sleep! Forgot the Boche (Germans) flying over at noon?" whispered Smitty.

"Just taunting us. Harmless."

"Ha! They were lining up targets for tonight, you know that. Close the door. "

Matt climbed under khaki blankets, tossed and turned, then sat upright. Katharine was on his mind; *writing will draw her closer*. By candlelight he searched his pack for pen and paper. Despite the faint sound of aircraft, he slipped into a reverie, trying to recall events since New York.

2

On June 15, 1918, moving in single file along the pier, men of the 112th Sanitation Battalion waved to teary-eyed well-wishers, some of whom had broken the line and rushed up as if to halt the steady procession of troops moving up the gangway. Longshoremen hoisted provisions to the deck where seamen unhooked pallets and sent back empty ropes. The New York skyline was a maze of building tops blocking any hint of sun; rain-filled clouds darkened the pier and brackish sea water lapped against the rusted hull.

Matt adjusted his pack and stepped on to the gangway. "Write home when you get across," urged a YMCA secretary, holding out three postcards for each man. Matt took them and stepped upward. The gangplank groaned under the load, its sway giving force to his emotional swings. Reaching the top, Matt paused, looked down the line of troops and cast a nostalgic eye on the civilian passing out cards. *Fool. Why didn't you stay with the 'Y?'*

"Keep a movin!" came a voice from below, followed by a surge upward that sent Matt sprawling on to the deck.

"Not so fast! What's the rush?" He moved forward along the ship's rail, eyes searching for an open hatch. Finding it, he descended to the lower deck and looked for his compartment. *Ah, there it is.* Walking inside he threw down the pack and hooked up his hammock. Others were doing the same. Matt blurted out, "Who could sleep in this rotten hole? I can hardly breathe. Is that oily smell from the engine room or the bilge? Let's bed down on deck!"

"Mind if I take the lower spot for my hammock?" asked Corporal Smith as he wiggled his way, pack and all, through the compartment hatch. His small head, sandy hair, and blinking eyes gave the impression of a raw recruit. "Smitty" was Matt's confidante, a foot shorter but a grade above, and the only man in the platoon who had been to college. Smitty "knew everything."

"How'll I get up and down that narrow ladder? You're nimbler than I," argued Matt.

"I'm a deep-sleeper. Afraid I'll tumble on to the deck in the middle of the night. C'mon, Matt. Be a pal. Besides, I outrank you. Never forget that."

"Pulling rank? So soon?" parried Matt, as he unhooked his hammock and headed out the hatch to carry out his first impulse. No one followed his lead, yet Matt didn't care. Being the youngest in a family of eleven made independent thinking a must for Matt's survival. He had learned to live by his wits. Walking into new situations, his brown eyes move up and down, right and left, while his mind tallies up profit and loss. Those eyes seemed able to pierce facade, and finding it, shear error from truth as scissors cut rough edges from a garment.

That's why he was a loner, despite his appearance and sense of humor. His great shock of black hair moved from his brow to the back of his head in tousled waves, giving him the appearance of a Hungarian prince. In fact, genealogies traced the Kingsbury line through England to one of Hungary's revered fourteenth century monarchs. During the American Civil War, his grandfather, Lt. General Henry Kingsbury, served in the Union Army. Matt's humor, bordering satire, seized upon contradiction and incongruence. When his remarks became too scathing, he would smother an embarrassed smile with his whole hand.

Out of sight behind the smokestack he unrolled several blankets on the wooden deck, stretched out a lanky frame, and lay wide awake allowing his thoughts to fold back upon themselves. Toward dusk, haze in the air cast the ship in lurid yellow light; the drowsy murmur of faint voices brought needed sleep. Before midnight, Matt was awakened by steps on the deck. He looked into the darkness and saw a pinprick of light widen as footsteps grew louder. It was Smitty. "Move aside! The stench below is too much." Matt obliged and then couldn't get back to sleep.

"Smitty!"

"What? I'm trying to sleep."

"I can't believe it," mused Matt. "One assassin's bullet sends France against Germany, pulls me away from Katharine, and lands us on this wretched deck."

"Fools! Fools! Not the likes of us. We're medics. Just think of it as a free trip to Europe. We'll see France inside out," opined Smitty.

3

Next morning at 6:00 a.m., the *Plassy* steamed out of New York harbor. Matt watched Miss Liberty pass to starboard as cold sea spray wet his face. *Will this be my last view?* The *Plassy* had been a British transport for 19 years, carrying troops to and from India. She was now on her first voyage as an American troopship, manned by English sailors, Portuguese waiters, and Indian deckhands. Matt watched them prepare the ship for open sea. The Indians seemed a ragged bunch, poor fellows who lived in the bowels of the ship. Folding hawsers, they scampered over the deck in bare feet with dirty rags wrapped around their heads as turbans. The sea turned choppy, the air foggy and damp. Smaller vessels faded from view, like spectral ghosts walking a pale sea. Before long the *Plassy* began laboring against heavy swells, and the captain ordered all troops below.

After a night of wrenching seasickness Matt returned to his haven behind the smokestack, his eyes following the *Plassy*'s churned wake. *Ah, we're not alone.* Scattered across a white-flecked sea were twelve transports and one battle cruiser in formation, patrolled overhead by an American zeppelin. Once they entered the Gulf Stream, the surging sea smoothed into a peaceful lake under bright sun. Other troops followed Matt, abandoning close quarters below for fresh air above. By day they watched English sailors load and unload a three-inch gun, the ship's only defense against submarines. By night they would huddle around cramped spaces on deck and bed down under overcoats. Matt, having secured the most favored spot, awoke when others shifted position. His covered legs pillowed their heads.

On the twelfth day a lighthouse was sighted off the coast of Scotland. The *Plassy* had safely passed the danger zone where attacks occurred. Others were not as fortunate. A wireless message received on the bridge reported one ship torpedoed and sunk 10 miles astern. Matt glanced out the porthole and was surprised to see land a short distance off starboard. He said to himself, *I'm sure every man from the colonel to the poorest Hindu coal-carrier feels an unspeakable thankfulness to God.*

As they steamed up the curving Firth of Clyde, a green peak broke through low-lying clouds. Then, at a blast of the ship's horn, legions of gulls perched on a great white rock leapt to the sky, regrouped, descended, and fluttered their wings. The beauty of rectangular fields of gold, green, and purple rising above the sea called forth admiration from men along deck rails. Through a pair of glasses Matt picked up a shepherd and his flock. *Bonny, bonny Scotland. You are wonderful!*

When he awoke next morning, the *Plassy* was tied up at a Glasgow pier; he hurriedly stuffed his pack and joined the Sanitation Battalion lined up to disembark. From the foot of the gangplank British officers marched them to a troop train waiting in the station not five minutes away. The train, small by

American standards, had little coaches divided into six compartments, each of which would hold six soldiers with overcoats, packs, and rations. A little old Scotsman gave the signal. Slowly the train moved out of the station along tracks lined with waving Scots who had emerged from nearby ironworks to bid Godspeed. Matt poked his head out the window and waved back.

Traveling at 35 mph, the train passed within 30 miles of London, turned southwest, and by midnight arrived at Winchester, famed for its great cathedral and King Arthur's Round Table. Men tumbled from their "cattle cars" in great relief and marched through the sleeping city in a column of twos. Except for a shaded lantern carried by a guide, the trip to the Rest Camp was made in darkness. For a while the men trudged in silence, but the cadence of hobnail boots striking cobblestone streets had a certain rhythm. Smitty started to whistle and all joined in. Their exuberance was soon dashed when the men reached Morn Hill and experienced an English Rest Camp for the first time—boards to sleep on, very little to eat, no rest.

A day later the troops boarded a train for Southampton where upon arrival they were herded into another English Rest Camp near the pier and given corned beef on hard biscuits. At 5:30 p.m. they embarked on *Queen Alexandra*, a long, thin craft that skimmed the channel at 25 knots, battering white caps. Nearly everyone, including Matt, lost his dinner. They disembarked at Cherbourg, marched to the city's railroad yards and were loaded, 37 men each, into small boxcars, crowded but glad to get out of the Rest Camp.

After detraining at Bourmont, headquarters of the 37th Division, Matt's unit marched 15 miles under blue skies and along empty roads in extreme heat and then climbed away from the lowlands. Reaching a ridge, Matt, along with Smitty and others, fell out from sheer exhaustion; they had had no lunch, and it was now 3:00 p.m. Next morning, after more corned beef and biscuits, they were on the move again, and by 10:00 p.m. reached Baccarat, a typical town in a valley on a small tributary of the Meuthe River. Trains of wounded soldiers, American and

French, often passed through on their way to a base hospital. Some of the medics were billeted in barracks, others in haylofts, and a few like Matt and Smitty, in old barns. The town was in total darkness, as were all French towns at night.

4

The sound of approaching aircraft jolted Matt out of his brown study. Within minutes, eight to ten bombs dropped on the town, four of which scored hits. One fell on a French home across the river, another across the street from Division Headquarters but neither did much damage. A third fell on a Signal Corps barrack, killing one man outright and fatally injuring three others, including a French soldier. A fourth landed 50 feet from Sanitation Train Headquarters, flinging shrapnel through tents into the flesh of men already wounded. US anti-aircraft guns filled the sky with bullets. The *put-put-put* of machine guns and boom of bigger guns grew louder. One explosion shook the earth and lit the sky dull red. Matt fell back from the doorway and dropped to his knees as if to hide under his helmet. At the sound of an ambulance being cranked up he raced over to see if any wounded had been carried to the triage point.

The following day, on a bright Sunday afternoon, Matt and Smitty joined a small procession making its way to the Cemetaire Militaire de Baccarat with four men prepared for burial. They would not rest alone. Matt counted 150 graves of Rainbow Division soldiers. Each grave was marked with a glass-encased picture of a ruined city with heavy clouds overhead, a rainbow shining through the clouds, and in its center the American flag. A French artist had tried to capture the meaning of their sacrifice. Matt bowed his head.

Several young women from the local glass works stood with the Americans, looking silently at the glass-encased pictures. One of them turned to Matt and said, "Our factory made those pictures. Messieurs visit us?"

Monday afternoon Matt made his way into town for a tour of the glass works. Old men were carting sand, young women blowing glass bubbles at the end of long pipes. *Where are the town youth? At the Front? Wounded? Killed by the Boche? We're not seeing France inside out, but empty.* As Matt left, the same young woman tossed her brunette head of curls toward a small cottage. "You come visit some evening, Monsieur?"

From Baccarat they proceeded by truck to Merviller, a small town located in a rich fruit-farming area only 6 miles from the Front and where was quartered the Ambulance Triage Station of the Rainbow Division. All ambulances from this sector, Matt learned, come through the station when making trips to the front and back. A record of each man in the ambulance is hurriedly jotted down, then the car sent to a field hospital 4 miles away in Baccarat. That evening Matt watched big guns flash across the northern sky. The roar was deafening. *So I am now at the Front*! He retrieved pen and paper and wrote Katharine:

> The town is no more secluded
> And the Boche calmly picks out his mark,
> Then a whizz and a flash, a bang and a crash
> And again the country is dark.
> And so it is in the moonlight
> When lovers in peaceable times
> Put out songs to their loved ones
> And pray for the old moon to shine
> But me for the rain and the darkness
> When all is hidden from view,
> For Boche don't bother our slumbers
> And my thoughts can run back to you.

Matt's ambulance was pressed into night supply duty; they must rush bacon and flour up to the 147th. The mud road passed through dark and lonely woods, but bursting star shells lit up the trucks, wagons, and troops on the road. They returned safely at midnight, only to discover a German aviator had been brought down near Merviller at dusk and carried to their triage. Matt stared at his lifeless form, a blond lieutenant in bloodied uniform lying by the side of the tent. Even a dead enemy is a person. Matt drew closer. A grotesque evil shrouded the corpse, an evil that sucks life out of a nation for reasons never clear.

Two weeks later Matt's unit left for Verdun. Every road was filled with artillery, trucks, and horses. Loaded in three trucks and three Red Cross Fords, the ambulance corpsmen made the best of a bad journey, bumping over roads, singing songs, yelling at infantry, eating and drinking provisions for the Front. Late at night, they reached Ricacourt and then turned into a wood full of shell holes. Matt quickly set up a canvas kitchen, camouflaging it with branches. The next day they were on the road again, starting, stopping, sleeping under a canopy of forest punctured by wayward shells. After three such days the convoy pulled into Brabant near the Front.

The weather turned cold. Matt put on two shirts, a coat, and a jerkin and then issued overcoats to shivering troops. At 7:00 p.m. three mortar shells whizzed by and dropped on a hill 500 feet away. Brabant was a mass of ruins; almost every building had been shelled. Yet shattered rooms, even a damaged church, provided space for field hospital work. Here they would bivouac.

To a soldier at the Front, mail from home was like momentary leave. Matt grabbed letters thrust in his direction and tore open the one with Katharine's handwriting. His eyes lingered on the last paragraph: "I remember our time together in church. It was then so quiet. There's something so peaceful about the early morning. I love you." The second letter, from the Columbus YMCA secretary, cautioned about moral wounds inflicted by war and foreign environments:

"Folks at home will suffer if you don't return just as you left. The `Y' keeps moving along, but we need you to care for the youth. We haven't anyone else like you."

Admonition mediated by acceptance drove Matt to his knees. Among the trees and out of eyeshot from comrades, Matt held the letter and pleaded, "Oh, Lord, make this letter an instrument for my regeneration in this land of war demons. Uncaged, they fill every place. They destroy foundations of character made back home. I have not gone unscathed. Wilt thou be near me, Savior, in my trials and temptations?"

By early November military lines of engagement had shifted. Matt's ambulance corps drove north to Deuterghen, Belgium, where the 145th Field Hospital had set up a triage to handle heavy casualties. Retreating Germans were creating havoc, tossing grenades into homes, shooting civilians at random. One day alone brought over six hundred wounded through the triage. Matt saw American, French, and German soldiers lying on litters, side by side with Belgian civilians. Worst off were old men, women, and children who had been caught between the two armies. He stood helpless as a Belgian mother dropped water into the blue lips of a six-year-old girl dying from shrapnel wounds. Her bluish face reminded him of the German aviator. *Why don't you do something?* He reached down to check her wounds and then stopped. *It's probably too late.*

A week later Matt wrote to Katharine from Deyrze, Belgium: "This is being written in a room of St. Henny College on a day memorable in the history of the world. At 11:00 o'clock this morning, the 11th month, the 11th day, the Armistice went into effect. I have read the terms of peace and hear of great celebrations in England. Reverently, I thank Him for this great day and for all that it means the wide world over."

5

Matt sailed into New York Harbor aboard a crowded troopship, welcomed by Miss Liberty with upraised torch. Matt needed that, for as tugboats nudged the liner pier-ward, he recognized no face or voice among the flag-waving crowd below, nor did any of the men of the 112th Sanitation Battalion. That would not happen until they reached Ohio a day later.

As the Battalion train pulled into Columbus Station, Matt's eyes ran up and down the platform. *There they are! Mother and Dad. With brother Harry. And yes. There's Katharine! They don't recognize me. Could six months change a man's face?*

"Ah, there he is," they cried out, as Matt broke ranks and rushed up. He fell into their embrace, pack and all, and then slipped out of the straps to lift Katharine in his arms. With a kiss he whispered, "How I missed you! I'll never leave this land again."

Rash promises come back to haunt those who make them. "A letter for you from the 'Y' secretary," said Matt's father, holding out a brownish envelope. Matt pocketed the unopened letter and read it that evening in the quietness of his room: "General Graves of the American Expeditionary Force in Siberia requests YMCA service to American troops and railway engineers living in harsh conditions. After returning to civilian life, will you go?" In one way the words came as a shock; in another, a relief. Ever since walking away from that Belgian mother and her child, he felt like a fugitive waiting to be caught. Moreover, the secretary's call strengthened a growing conviction that he could no longer live a self-serving life in the teeth of human suffering. Faces of shattered forms lying on litters in cold tents would not go away.

Matt had forgotten how beautiful Katharine was. She looked lovelier than ever dressed for the

Christmas Eve service at Old Stone. Her golden hair, parted at the top and swirling around her cheeks like a picture frame, set off blue eyes that probed Matt's thoughts. Her tall, slender frame belied an inner strength. Matched by a Roman nose that pointed resolutely toward a chosen path, Katharine's whole demeanor exuded confidence and poise. Matt knew his plans for their future could not be visionary. They talked together on the way home from the candlelight service. Matt mentioned in vague terms the YMCA opening.

"But if you go on staff at the 'Y,' won't it delay our wedding? They don't pay a living wage. Do you want me to keep working?"

"That's not the only problem, Katharine." Matt was searching for a way to explain. "The letter Dad gave me at the station mentioned something else. An assignment overseas."

"Where?"

"Siberia. In the far eastern corner of Russia."

"Siberia?" There was a note of alarm, even fear in Katharine's voice.

"Yes. Don't you remember? The American Expeditionary Force arrived in Vladivostok several months ago. Troop morale is down. Red Cross workers can do little. They're tied up with wounded Czechs flowing into the city from the eastern Russian front. Thousands, literally. An American general invited the 'Y' over to entertain US troops."

"Matt," pleaded Katharine, "you've been away all these months. You know how anxious I've been. I thought you wanted to marry and settle down. Now you want to leave again and put yourself in harm's way. "

"Would you consider going with me? The commander requested help from the YWCA."

"Me? Go to Siberia? I'm a homebody."

"Katharine, remember what we heard tonight. 'Comfort ye, comfort ye my people.' God comforts people through His servants. You and I can be those servants in Siberia. In France, the 'Y' was there when I needed help. Who wrote me when I was down? The 'Y.' Those special religious services in France. Who arranged them? The 'Y.'" There was no anger in Matt's piercing eyes, only pleading, but when he leaned over and kissed Katharine's wet cheek, she turned away.

6

Warm weather brought hints of green to lifeless branches. Snow had turned to hard rain, churning streets into mud washboards. A tall civilian made his way through the wet furrows and headed for U.S. Army headquarters, Vladivostok. He paused when the path opened a spectacular view of the harbor. By their flags he could recognize the British cruiser *Suffolk,* the *Brooklyn,* flagship of the United States' Asian fleet, the Chinese *Hai Jung,* and the warships *Iwami, Asahi,* and *Asakage* from the island empire of Japan. Around them, like courtiers in waiting, rusted merchants with hoisted colors lay at anchor. What are they doing here? Then he remembered the orientation lecture: the British had brought economic relief to prevent a Russian military collapse, the Americans had come to strengthen Russian efforts at self-defense, guard sectors of the Trans-Siberian railroad, and rescue a corps of Czech soldiers trying to break out of the eastern front; the Chinese, to maintain the status quo along the Russian-Manchurian border; the Japanese, to help the Allies any way possible.

To the orderly on duty he turned over his card, *Matt Kingsbury, YMCA secretary-on-assignment*.

"I believe the General is in. He asked me to come."

"This way."

General Graves stood up as Matt entered the office. Without his military insignia, broad-brimmed hat and high leather boots, Graves could pass as a bespectacled college professor. Col. Styer, seated to Graves' left on a canvas-covered folding chair, also rose and held out his hand. "Welcome. We're glad the YMCA has come. And of course, the YWCA," said Graves and then introduced Styer.

"Mr. Kingsbury, this is Col. Styer, my adjutant. I was out inspecting troops when you arrived last month. Have you settled in? Are YWCA volunteers finding their quarters bearable? How's the canteen coming along?"

Two officers standing together, with silver stars and eagle insignia on lapels reminded Matt of his erstwhile Private status and kept him at a respectful distance. His eyes avoided theirs and fell on the huge horizontal world map behind them. Siberia lay in the center. Two colored ribbons, red and blue, marked the location of 27th and 31st Infantry units. Matt regained his composure: "We're coping, but the women, including my fiancée, are sick of all this rain and mud. Since we opened the canteen last week, men are coming every night; they enjoy the games, and even the bookshelves are emptying fast."

"How's troop morale?" asked Graves, returning to his canvas chair. "It's hard for me to judge. No one wants to give a general bad news."

"Could be better," replied Matt. "They dislike the command's ban on liquor. But it's safer that way. Typhus is running rampant, and enlisted men, if not sick, get into brawls with sailors or Czechs. The midnight curfew is a good idea."

"Our greatest problem lies outside Vladivostok," broke in Styer, standing to his feet and going over to the map. "Bolshevik bands roaming the countryside are getting near guard units to the north."

"Which units?" interrupted Graves, putting on his glasses as he looked closer to the map.

"Ours. Troops from the 31st," answered Styer.

"Ah, the 31st," continued Graves, "guarding American engineers scattered along the Amur track as far out as Verkne-Udinsk. Also protecting Czech troops on their way to Vladivostok, are they not?"

"Yes, but Bolsheviks keep their distance, so men don't take them seriously. Frankly, after the armistice our troops see no danger from war prisoners, no need to protect military stores or aid the Czechs. On my last inspection, half the men were gone—out fishing and hunting in nearby forests. Siberia is a fisherman's paradise. They catch salmon with bare hands," offered Styer.

"Have you contacted our railroad engineers yet, Mr. Kingsbury?" interjected Graves.

"No. But I would like to."

"Before turning over more arms to Czarist troops, I plan a trip to the West. If General Semenov is anything like his eastern counterpart, Admiral Kolchak, Russian peasants will not follow him. Would you like to go with us?"

"Yes, General. Very much so."

"I'll arrange to have you in my coach. But first, I want you to meet the commandant of Japanese forces in Vladivostok, Captain Ken Nakajima. He has expressed reservations about arming Kolchak's troops; they rob and murder innocent Russian peasants. Why don't you invite him to the canteen? It's for all Allied forces. He may want his troops to use your services."

Several days later at Japanese headquarters Matt was ushered before Captain Nakajima. Seated to the right was an interpreter whom Nakajima disdained to use most of the time. When English nuances proved incomprehensible, Nakajima would turn reluctantly to his right, whisper into the interpreter's ear, cup a hand in front of his own ear to listen, then face his guest, saying, "Ah....so, I see, I see."

Ken Nakajima was not the typical Japanese officer, though his appearance suggested otherwise: high cheekbones, ruddy complexion, cropped hair, ramrod back, and small, stout legs wrapped in army-green puttees. At the age of nineteen he had enlisted in the army and was eventually posted to Siberia. There he rapidly rose in the ranks because of an uncanny ability to adapt to bad situations, make the best of them and turn them to advantage. Absolute devotion to country stood in counterpoise to his versatility. These qualities thrust him into the rank of captain at the age of 25.

At the end of formalities, Matt said, "If you have a minute, I'd like you to go with me to the canteen. I'm on my way there now. General Graves is also coming. It's not five minutes away. It's for all Allied troops." Nakajima followed Matt through canteen doors, bowing to everyone. His eyes fell on a tall, beautiful young woman with blonde hair, wearing a YWCA cap. Matt walked over, stood beside her and spoke:

"My fiancée—Katharine Howe. Katharine, this is Captain Nakajima."

Katharine made a short bow, saying, "Hello sir, may I get you something to drink?"

Within minutes General Graves came to their table and sat down as Katharine passed coffee around. Taking cup in hand, General Graves faced Nakajima and expressed appreciation for Japan's role in the Allied intervention, then left with a challenge. "Semenov and Kolchak are supported by Japan. Their actions will cause resentment by the Siberian people, not only against Japan, but against all nations taking part in the intervention. The Siberian people are sure to reason that the presence of foreign soldiers makes it possible for Cossacks to rob, beat, and murder men, women, and children. The acts of these Cossacks under the protection of foreign troops can do nothing but help the Bolshevik cause. Their atrocities will be remembered by the Russian people for years to come. We will have no one to blame but ourselves. You are now in a position to express yourself to the Tokyo government, Captain Nakajima. I trust you will do so."

As the General spoke, Nakajima kept his head down. Slowly it came up as if to offer a defense and then went down again. The only words Matt heard were, "For samurai you ask impossible."

7

Matt pulled himself out of the wool sleeping bag, threw cold water over his face, grabbed a few belongings, and rushed out the door. Running through the station he saw a uniformed US officer standing by Coach Four. "I thought you might not make it," yelled Styer above hissing steam. Both clambered aboard and found their compartment next to that of General Graves. With a jolt the Trans-Siberian Express moved out of the station.

The grass country through which they passed revealed unusual fertility. Near Nikolsk, the land was a rolling prairie planted in wheat. From his coach window Matt looked in vain for a typical Russian farmhouse. What came into view were clusters of clapboard houses where peasants live in community. From one house he could see a small group walking with long scythes and rakes. In fields were babushka-covered women stacking hay in wooden enclosures. "Why stack hay away from the houses?" he asked Styer.

"Few peasants have the luxury of a barn. The wooden stalls will be dismantled and moved to another hayfield when animals need a fresh supply."

Gradually grain fields gave way to mile after mile of pine and birch forest. Along the 5,600-mile Trans-Siberian Railroad the most difficult stretch to keep in operation runs from Karimskaya to Irkutsk, which they were about to enter. The express crossed the Trans-Baikal plateau and went around the southern tip of Lake Baikal. Their compartment went from light to dark as the train burrowed through 38 mountain tunnels. The grey lake turned white at the edge and extended to the moving train. Matt realized it was frost on the ground; except for July, the Trans-Baikal plateau is covered with permafrost. Only the stout-hearted can brave the climate.

Midway lies the junction town Verkne-Udinsk where the great caravan route extending from Kalgan in the Mongolian desert ends. In 1919, it took 40 days for camel trains to make the trip. Verkne-Udinsk was Western Headquarters for several battalions of the U.S. 27th Infantry, assigned by the Allied Railroad Agreement to protect this section of the railroad, tunnels and all. In command was Colonel Morrow who had the distinction of being the first US officer to contact the notorious General Semenov. Robust, with leather face made tougher still by icy winds from the Siberian steppe, Morrow could be genial and stern. He could also bluff if occasion demanded.

Graves, Styer and Matt were met by Morrow when they detrained at Verkne-Udinsk. After inspecting the camp and Morrow's troops, they relaxed in the officers' mess. The subject quickly turned to Semenov: "Just last week Semenov's troops came into our area and arrested some railway employees," began Morrow.

"On what grounds?"

"They were Bolsheviks."

"What did you do?"

"Notified Semenov that such arrests could not be made in my sector without criminal evidence."

"How did that sit with Semenov?"

"He was horrified that a foreigner on Russian soil could tell him what he could or could not do, then threatened to come and arrest more employees."

"And?" asked Matt, intrigued at Morrow's boldness.

"I told Semenov his armored train would be blown to perdition if it approached Verkne-Udinsk. We then sandbagged 37mm guns on both sides of the track, and waited for him to appear. He didn't."

Early next morning the trio bid farewell to Morrow and boarded the train for Ikurtsk. Eighty miles west of Verkne-Udinsk the train reached Lake Baikal and ran close to the shore for about 180 miles. Their eyes took in the vast sweep of this 400-mile-long, gray body of water, varying in width from 20 to 60 miles, with an area of 60,000 square miles and an extreme depth of 6,500 feet. 4500-foot snow-capped mountains stood as majestic sentinels around the lake.

Situated on the Angara River 40 miles downstream from the lake was Ikurtsk, the metropolis of central Siberia with a tragic history. In Czarist times, prisoners exiled to Siberia were assembled in Irkutsk for confinement or surveillance. As the Americans walked around town, they caught sight of prisoners with cumbersome chains fastened around their ankles. On the end of each chain a large ball was fastened, to be carried when walking.

After leaving Irkutsk, they passed through a heavily wooded section for about 400 miles and then approached the great Siberian steppes that rose beyond Krasnoyarsk, a town established in 1628 on the banks of the Yenessei River. Styer explained the town's significance: "Those barracks at the end of the town were a prison camp for German and Austrian soldiers captured on the Eastern front. The treatment of these men was a disgrace to modern civilization. After the armistice, the Russians did not free them. Or feed them. They languished in squalor, kept alive by a young Swedish woman from the town who regularly brought food and clothing to the camp."

Semenov, hearing that General Graves had arrived in Krasnoyarsk, sent for him immediately. Graves and Matt, with Styer in the lead, were escorted by a phalanx of troops to Cossack headquarters. There, hunched in a large wooden chair resembling a medieval throne, sat General Semenov in an oversized coat decorated with faded insignia. Except for the bushy mustache drooping over his decayed teeth, the appearance was Mongolian, not Russian.

Semenov was a Cossack, born in the small village of Kuranzka, on the middle reaches of the Onon river in southern Trans-Baikal territory. Fired with tales of ancient Mongol greatness, he developed into a bold, brutal frontiersman and considered himself a latter-day Genghis Khan, riding at the head of the nomads to save the Czar. Only 29 years old, he was fond of keeping one hand thrust into his coat and always carried Napoleon's *Maxims* in his pocket. Dominated to a large extent by his mistress, he spent hundreds of thousands of rubles upon her. Semenov ruled as dictator of Chita, a city in the southeast where he looted banks and custom houses at will. He shipped military supplies to Chita on trains without paying freight or duty and sold goods to the civilian population in so-called *Semenov Stores*.

Lacking moral principle, Semenov murdered whole villages. One such village near Morrow's sector was suspected of harboring Bolshevik sympathizers. When Semenov troops reached the village, the inhabitants apparently tried to escape. But soldiers shot them down in cold blood, men, women and children, and left their bodies in open fields. Morrow took both a Frenchman and a Japanese to verify this massacre. They signed Morrow's report.

Semenov's ferocity toward the weak was matched by his servility to the strong. He let nothing interfere with his compliance to Japanese wishes and kept military operations never far from Japanese troops. He could not last a week in Siberia without their protection.

In Graves' brief encounter with Semenov they discussed plans for securing the Trans-Siberian Railroad, and how to guarantee safe passage for Czech soldiers making their way to Vladivostok. In his farewell, Graves expressed his hope for Semenov: "General, in the West we have the Ten Commandments. Whatever religious code you adhere to, may I encourage you to follow the laws of right and wrong?"

8

Semenov worked hand-in-glove with Rozanoff, a Cossack general whose criminal acts brought him to the same depths as Semenov. At Kranoyarsk, Graves was shown a directive Rozanoff had sent his troops, dated March 27, 1919. Translated into English it read:

"After securing villages previously occupied by partisans, insist on getting leaders of the movement. Where you cannot get the leaders, but know of their presence, shoot one of every ten villagers."

Such were the acts of Czarist hatchet men. Matt's sympathy for the Allied cause turned to outrage. Their trip confirmed the General's greatest fear: Japan and the Allies were arming the worst criminals in Siberia. Russian peasants would choose to side with the Bolsheviks. Allied support of Kolchak and Semenov was not weakening the Bolshevik cause but strengthening it. This would destabilize the region and prove just cause for Japanese forces' staying on after the Allies left.

From Krasnoyarsk, Graves, Styer, and Matt boarded a train going due west to Omsk. An American officer, Colonel Emerson, was there to greet them. He had come ahead to take inventory of material shipped for railway repair. As they climbed into a seven-passenger Cadillac sent by flat car for the general, Graves queried Emerson,

"How's the mobilization coming? Reports have it that Kolchak's command has 20,000 men in the north, 31,000 in the center, 50,000 in the south, all prepared to crush the Bolsheviks."

"Looks good on paper," said Emerson. "From what I hear, those forces are nothing but a retreating mob. That's why you're here. Ask Kolchak's commander-in-chief for permission to witness the mobilization."

They drove immediately to the commander's headquarters on the outskirts of Omsk, who, unfortunately, made a counter- proposal:

"I regret you cannot go directly south to Petropavlosk. That route is clogged with troops. Besides, Admiral Kolchak is due any day. Go by train to Ishim, then motor to Petropavlosk."

Emerson had the Cadillac hoisted back on the flatcar, then added several coaches to the train. These would sleep and feed the American contingent now comprised of three officers, Matt, and 25 US infantry escorts. The 160-mile trip to Ishim took 32 hours. Most of the time was spent on sidings waiting for troop trains to pass, curiously, in the other direction. Matt shut his eyes to the spectacle but was too anxious to sleep. Each motionless hour seemed an eternity.

At Ishim they were met by an English officer assigned to Kolchak's troops. After formal handshakes he steered the Americans away from Petropavlosk: "General, I beg of you not to go across there, as the Bolsheviks will capture you, and that will spoil all we have accomplished here."

Whereupon Graves sought out the Russian commander in Ishim, requesting Russian troops to bolster the American platoon. The reply was cold and abrupt: "The risk is too great. I have no soldiers I can trust as your escort."

Crestfallen, the travelers retraced steps to their coaches waiting on a siding near the Ishim station. "I'm beginning to wonder if this Russian army is a myth. We must go see for ourselves," said Graves. Off came the Cadillac. An American flag was attached to the radiator, and from a vertical rod the two-star flag of a Major General unfurled. The four men with an interpreter and one infantryman climbed aboard. All except the infantryman strapped pistols to their sides; he held his rifle in readiness. They left at 7:00 p.m. on a furrowed road going southeast to Peterpavlosk. After driving 63 miles through darkness, the better part of wisdom sent them into an oat-field to await daylight.

At 2:00 a.m. they were awakened by a Russian on horseback galloping up and shouting, "Who are you? What are you doing here?" The interpreter's explanation worked magic; their torch showed the Russian's glowering face turn to a warm smile:

"Won't you spend the rest of the night in our village? It's an honor to entertain an American general."

Graves politely declined: "We must move on at daybreak."

At sunrise they were off. Before long they came to the Ishim River where the gutted road vanished. Peasant men, women, and children circled the Cadillac. Hershey chocolate bars, essence of American diplomacy, worked wonders. On to a crudely fashioned raft the Cadillac was inched, then pulled across the 300-yard-wide river by cable. By 10:00 a.m., the car came to a village 30 miles from Petropavlosk.

All eyes scanned the horizon, searching for the chimera Kolchak army. On the trip only three Russian soldiers had been seen. Suddenly there were sounds of movement as a Russian officer in full regalia came strutting out of a light blue clapboard house. Village idlers, old men, and children formed his retinue. "Welcome!" he said, throwing his arms around General Graves. "I am General Sakharoff, commandant at Petropavlosk. Word that you might come reached me yesterday. Please be our guests in Petropavlosk. Before that, rest here awhile. The priest wants you to come to the church for cake and wine."

"Indeed," replied Graves. "And you be our guest the next 30 miles. Let's ride together into Petropavlosk." The offer pleased Sakharoff. After finishing refreshments at the parsonage, they bid farewell to villagers and returned to the Cadillac. In the back seat, with interpreter between, Graves turned toward Sakharoff, raising his voice above the car engine:

"Where are your troops?"

"I have none."

"How do you expect to start an offensive in two weeks?"

"An offensive? If one is planned, you know more about it than I."

There was nothing more to see; the Russian army didn't exist. What did exist were disillusioned Cossack troops moving *en masse* away from Bolshevik lines, not toward them. Thirty trains passing east, while Graves' party traveled west and waited on sidings for them to pass, bore thousands of disorganized troops, some wounded, most unarmed, but to a man convinced they were fighting a lost cause. They were going home. Kolchak could fight his own battles.

9

The Trans-Siberian Express picked up speed in the lowlands as the travelers approached Omsk on the return to Vladivostok. Major General Ivanoff-Rinoff, commander of all Siberian Cossacks, came to meet Graves and his party at the Omsk station. He was to be promoted the next day by Admiral Kolchak himself. Could they stay overnight and attend the ceremony?

"Well, uh..., yes," said Graves. He would witness the charade if only to lay eyes on the infamous Kolchak.

While the American trio toured Omsk, news came of a troop train arriving at Kolumzino, across the river from Omsk. Rumors swept like wildfire through the city: "Stay away. Sick and wounded from the front. Most have typhus."

"Let's see for ourselves. Russian rumors bode something worse," remarked Graves, as he turned toward the river. It was no rumor. Sick and wounded troops returning from the front had been laid in boxcars without any accommodations. Many were too ill to help themselves. Only one nurse for every five hundred men. No arrangements for food. Limited water in canteens. The trio glanced into the first boxcar and saw two dead men in a heap on the floor. A third was dying while a sick comrade held his head and tried to give him water. Many of the sick had managed to crawl out of the cars. In utter exhaustion they were sprawled on the ground by the train, a helpless mass of humanity. These soldiers had given their lives fighting for the Kolchak cause. Yet Kolchak supporters, men and women alike, would not come to their aid. Words from the Bible came to Matt as they walked away from the pitiful scene: "Behold all ye who pass by! See if there be any sorrow like unto my sorrow."

Shortly after lunch the following day, Graves, Styer, and Matt made their way to a park near the Orthodox Church where festivities for the promotion ceremony had already begun. A band was playing and a thousand people dancing. Until dignitaries arrived, the Americans mingled with those on the park perimeter, then circumvented the crowd and entered the church. The center aisle was cordoned off for the procession. Matt was struck by the pathos of Eastern art—church walls decorated with icons portraying Christ on the Via Dolorosa.

The procession moved down the aisle, gold cross lifted high, choir singing, a priest holding the Bible, followed by two officers in dress uniform. After solemnly declaring fealty to God, His church and the Russian people, Ivanoff-Rinoff knelt while Admiral Kolchak commissioned him Lt. General. When Ivanhoff arose, Kolchak kissed both his cheeks, proclaimed him a Russian patriot and presented him a gold sword.

Matt sat silently, his eyes moving up and down, from icon to general, who, chest emblazoned with medals, took the sword and clasped it to his breast. In its scabbard the golden sword was an elongated cross. Now, above the proceedings, Matt's eyes fixed on Christ's thorned brow, his knees bent under the Cross. The enormity of the charade, the stark contrast was too much. Anger mounted. He must rise. *Stop! For Christ's sake you must arrest this man, not commission him!* But Matt sat stupefied, unable to utter a word.

Leaving the church before anyone could recognize their US army insignia, Graves turned to Styer, "When I get back to Vladivostok, I'll see the American consul and Japanese commandant. Peasants don't go over to the Bolsheviks because of any economic theory. They are driven. By terror. From Csarists like Semenov and Rinoff —the very ones Allies came to help. This travesty must end."

10

The US Expeditionary Force left Siberia for the United States on March 31, 1920, eighteen months after General Graves arrived. No one, least of all Graves, believed Allied efforts had brought lasting peace to Siberia. To the contrary, Bolsheviks were coming eastward at an alarming rate, while more and more Japanese troops dug in to checkmate them.

Two weeks before the US departure, Matt recruited an army chaplain to perform his and Katharine's wedding ceremony in this memorable setting. Part of the base mess was cordoned off, seats rearranged, a table spread with linen cloth, and a portable organ opened. From a supply kit the chaplain unfolded his vestments and then took out silver vessels with bread and wine for communion. The few guests invited, including Captain Nakajima, signed the guest book. Nakajima paused for a moment and then wrote in his Japan address.

Matt and Katharine stood before the robed chaplain. His words of admonition, only partially understood, puzzled Nakajima: "Will you love her, comfort her, honor her, and keep her?" Matt's pledge to Katharine, "I give you this ring as a symbol of my love, and with all that I am, and all that I have, I honor you," raised another question. A relationship between husband and wife, a relationship that spells out duties and responsibilities, that Nakajima could understand. *But Matt pledges to honor Katharine, to cherish her, to love her, even to submit to her out of reverence for his Lord Christ.* Nakajima's thoughts took flight from that makeshift chapel to his Nagano home where woman's place is in the home. The character for wife is woman-holding-broom. Even the character for tranquility pictures woman-inside-house. She is to surrender herself to husband and family. And if required, annihilate herself for her husband that he might annihilate himself for his master, and that master in turn might annihilate himself for Heaven. A daughter of the samurai must go through sacrificial stages for father, then husband, and finally son. A wife is not to be coddled but to serve a cause greater than herself, even at the sacrifice of her individuality.

Nakajima's eyes focused on what came next. The couple was kneeling, taking bread, and drinking wine from the chaplain's cup. Just as he had sipped *sake* with his bride. *Now what is the chaplain saying?* "This is my blood of the New Testament, which is shed for you for the remission of sins." *Why the negative? Sake speaks of celebration, happiness, not forgiveness.* The ceremony over, Nakajima lingered briefly and then filed out past the chaplain and smiling couple. "Best of luck," he whispered, and added, "Sayonara." Nakajima eventually made his way to Manchuria; Matt and Katharine, to Ohio.

11

A lone figure hastened over winding mountain paths, then descended to a plain checkered with green wheat and dark sod. Smoke wreaths rose gently from thatch-roofed homes nestled together in the upper reaches of the Chikuma River. At a turn in the path the tired traveler paused to take in the view. He took off an empty packsack, wiped his brow. *How will he tell Fumiko?* All that work they did together—crouched over paddies, wading in black mud, preparing the soil, thrusting down rice shoots, cutting ripe grain, storing it in bundles, slapping them on mats to separate chaff, hauling sacks to market. He pulled out the few *yen* his crop had yielded, counting them again in disbelief. *And they say next month's price will be lower.* The Great Depression of the West had come East. Exports dwindled and many people were out of work. *That settles it, Yuki must give up any thought of high school.*

At the corner of the last paddy, Ichiro, brother of Ken Nakajima, stopped to look at a grave marker above the family burial plot. It read, "Nakajima, man of strength." *Above my grave no priest could write that. He'll have to write, "Nakajima, man of weakness."* Could he live down the shame? The whole village knew in his blood ran that of Emperor Toba, who in a struggle for power with Emperor Go-Shirakawa, was sent into exile in 1158. During the Warring States period of the fifteenth century, the Nakajima family fled to this mountain fastness, out of harm's way. They had backed the wrong feudal lord. Deservedly, his clan was left in Nagano to fend for themselves, abandoned and forgotten. All those swords and daggers, sheathed in bamboo with the clan's crest embossed in gold on the handles, hanging in the dust-covered godown. *What are they?* Reminders of a glorious tradition lost through bad decisions.

Fumiko greeted Ichiro with a letter in hand: "From your brother Ken in Manchuria. He's offering room, board, and high school tuition if Yuki will help raise watchdogs for the Kwantung Army."

After supper the Nakajima family gathered around the central hearth to go over this unexpected offer. Ichiro began: "You don't have to go, son. You can help in the fields. I'll keep you busy."

"Are we sure Uncle Ken can get me into high school?"

"No. But we know you can't enter a Nagano one. If rice prices rise, we might scrape together enough for trade school."

"If Uncle Ken can't get me in a Changchun high school, may I return?"

"Of course."

"I'll go."

After packing belongings and bidding farewell to friends, Yuki stepped into a rickshaw. Ichiro and Fumiko followed in one behind until they reached Niigata Harbor. Their lives had been driven by necessity and Fumiko's face showed it: tanned by rice-planting in open paddies, wrinkled by squinting in winds from Mt. Asama, reddened by Nagano's severe winter. Holding one of Yuki's bundles, she dutifully walked behind father and son. Ichiro steeled himself for this moment and, like a good samurai, held his head high, walking resolutely, showing no emotion as they helped Yuki carry his belongings up the gangway. It was a small packet bound for Dairen. They grasped Yuki's hand saying, "*Itte irrasshai*," go and come back.

The five-day crossing of the Sea of Japan went without incident; Uncle Ken was standing at the dock to welcome his nephew; they boarded a train for Changchun and the Nakajima home. The erstwhile soldier-of-fortune was engaged in activities related to the Japanese presence. For one, raising dogs to guard nearby military installations had become profitable. Local youth were using ingenious tactics for raiding food depots, many of which kept rice provisions in open sheds. "What brought you here in the first place," Yuki queried Uncle Ken, as they finished their first evening meal together.

"In 1918, I went to Siberia with Imperial troops fighting Russian Bolsheviks. We were part of an international force. Then in 1925, when the Japanese army withdrew, I was deactivated but stayed on to work with Mitsubishi Foods. That is, until the Bolsheviks overran eastern Siberia and expropriated foreign firms; the company transferred its main operation to Changchun in 1927. I work for the company by day, but teach high school seniors by night. But first let me introduce Changchun to you and explain why we are here.

12

"Changchun serves as the northeast center of government, education and commerce. After the Manchurian Incident last year, as you may remember, Pu-yi, the last emperor of China, was installed here as puppet regent of the new Japanese colony. We live in the educational center of the city; down a few blocks is Harbin University, and to the rear of campus stands a Shinto shrine where Japanese come on festival days."

"Japanese festivals in China?" asked Yuki.

"Of course. Japanese people come on New Year's Day, the autumn or spring equinoxes, the May doll festival, etc. On the temple grounds I do my tutorials in a Japanese style house with *tatami*, straw mats, sliding doors and everything."

"Tutorials? Like back home?"

"Exactly. Japanese residents, mostly business people and bureaucrats, asked me to do it. They want their children to pass university entrance exams when they return to Japan."

"Mind if I audit?"

"Not at all."

Today, after kennel chores Yuki walks several blocks to the university gate, goes through, turns right to a forested area, jumps across a narrow stream, and comes into a clearing. Before him stands a medium-sized *torii*, a red arch supported by two circular columns, beyond which is the local Shinto Shrine. To the right is a large room with an entryway jammed with two dozen pair of *geta* (wooden clogs*). Ah,* he thought, *class has begun.* He removes his clogs, steps up, slides the paper doors aside, and sits down on *tatami* mats. Uncle Ken is just beginning.

Boys have come dressed in black kimono, hair cropped short, sitting with folded legs. Uncle Ken walks among students trying to write Japanese characters with a thin bamboo brush. "Ouch!" yells one boy, as Ken taps his hand with a birch-rod.

"Not up-and-down. Other way! Down-and-up! Curve to the right! Flatten your brush to spread the ink!"

"Yes, sir," replies the cowed student and tries again, this time pleased with his flourishes.

Next Ken turned to ancient history. "Class! I asked you to check encyclopedias to find out where the word *Nippon* originated."

A student at the front stood to his feet. "Right here in China. Looking from southeast out over the ocean, the Chinese knew a large island group lay in the east, beyond the horizon. They called it, 'Islands from where the sun rises' or *Nippon*, which means "origin of the sun.""

"Correct. But how do we get from the word *Nippon* to the word *Japan*? Who knows?"

A hand went up, and another youth stood to his feet to recite: "Marco Polo came from Italy over the silk road to China in the thirteenth century.

"What Polo learned about our islands he reported to the West, but in doing so mis-pronounced Nippon as *Japon*. Thus Western nations call our country *Japan*."

"Next, who knows the meaning of our national flag. Can you explain it? How about you?" said Ken, pointing to a youth in the third row.

"I understand the sun in the center represents Nippon, and the rays emanating from it signify Japan's worldwide influence."

"Yes, rays from the sun flash out 360 degrees, that is, around the whole world," answered Ken. "In the same way Japan's light must shine to every corner of the earth, and bring about *hakko ichiu*, all nations under one roof. Let me read what emperor Jimmu said in our eighth-century *Nihongi*, Japan Chronicles: `Thereafter may the capital be extended to the whole land under heaven and as far as the Emperor's rule extends, may there be a single household.' So it is Japan's destiny to bring benevolent rule to benighted lands like China. See how Chinese life has improved in Manchuria!"

At the next session Nakajima dwelt on *Shinto*, a religion intrinsic to Japan's national character. Pointing to the red-columned *torii*, he began. "The Chinese were the first to name our national religion. We never gave it a name or studied it; few wrote books about it. The Chinese called it *Shinto* (way of the gods). And who are the gods? Notice in this shrine there are no objects of worship. Only this bronze mirror. Why? It symbolizes the human heart, which when placid and clear, reflects the very image of the divine. Thus, when you stand before a shrine to worship, you see yourself. As Professor Nitobe says, this act of worship is tantamount to what Socrates said, 'Know thyself.' Yet, for us 'knowing thyself' is not the individual you but 'you' as an integral part of the nation, melded together by the gods. The 'you' worshipped includes our ancestors whose lineage is traced to the imperial dynasty. Nitobe said, 'To the average Japanese, Japan is more than land and soil from which to mine copper or reap grain. It is the sacred abode of the gods, the spirits of our forefathers. To him the emperor is more than a political ruler; he is the bodily representative of heaven and earth, blending in his person heaven's power and its mercy.'"

"If we worship ourselves, who are the gods? What role do they play?" asks a bewildered student staring at the mirror.

"The gods set us apart as a distinct race, linked to nature and each other through the medium of their ubiquitous presence. Over 260 gods are mentioned in the *Nihongi*: gods of the mountains, the sea, the harvests, the plains, etc. But that's only the beginning. There are millions of gods. You, class, are man-gods, not by birth or language but by essential oneness with ancestral gods. And as members of the Japanese race, you are to nourish your *yamato-damashi*, old Japan spirit. You have a national mission—to bring all of Asia under one roof. It is a just cause. It brings East Asians together, delivering them from bolshevism and anarchy, driving out Western colonialists. The Kwantung army's action last year was for this express purpose: pacifying the region. We do not want the destruction of China but her prosperity and progress."

"When you say 'national mission,'" continued the student, looking from the mirror to Nakajima, "do you mean we're here in Changchun because the emperor willed it? How do we know our presence is for the good of China? I see few prosperous Chinese in my neighborhood. Aren't we exploiting them? And that brings up the point that is troubling me. How do we distinguish good from evil? What is our standard? How do Western people discern right from wrong?"

"Western nations," replied Nakajima, "seek answers to such questions from the church. Or they leave value choices to individual conscience. Their governments concern themselves only with preserving public order. Not so Japan. In a drive to become modern after the Restoration of 1868, our leaders based control over the people on internal values rather than external laws. And those internal values flowed from the institution of the emperor. The Mikado combined in his person spiritual and political sovereignty over the people. We have never had an ecclesiastical authority to which the emperor was subject."

The student, still standing, pressed his case. "But sir, since the 1868 Restoration, there have been people's rights movements in Japan, such as during the 1920s."

"Yes, but those movements were only to define the limits of people's rights. And they never questioned traditional Confucian views about loyalty and filial piety. The Meiji Restoration brought prestige and power together in the emperor. Thereafter, definitions of truth, morality, and beauty were handed down by officials who gave loyal service to the emperor. The Japanese state has always had a monopoly on the right to determine values. That is why our first Japanese Parliament was not convened until Emperor Meiji so desired. The emperor is over law, not under it." Yuki's head was reeling by the time Uncle Ken's lecture ended.

Ken used the next session for explaining essential Asian thought. With broad brush strokes he painted large Chinese characters on great white sheets of paper, then broke each character down into simple, familiar icons. From them, to the astonishment of the class, he lifted grand themes of Asian philosophy like a pearl diver rising to the surface with her trove.

"Class! When you learned Chinese characters, you broke them down into smaller parts or components. All characters contain these components, arranged to convey different meanings. They represent objects of nature, such as the sun, moon, tree, sky, rain, and water. Also, they are parts of the human body, such as the hands, feet, heart, eyes, mouth, back, and legs."

"I guess that tells us that ancient Chinese people learned about life from nature," suggested a sympathetic student.

"Good thinking," answered Ken. "Do not Chinese characters themselves reinforce an East Asian man-in-nature view of life?"

Uncle Ken's third lesson showed where all this was going—*Bushido,* code of the warrior. He began with a summary statement:

"The word *Bushido* is comprised of three components: *military, knight,* and *way.* It is the accepted code of morality by which a samurai lives. It speaks of duty, obligation, honor, decorum, loyalty, self-control. Many of our proverbs come from samurai-based historical episodes. Such as *Bushi no nasake*, a warrier's compassion, *Bushi wa kuwanedo, takayoji,* the samurai glories in honorable poverty, or *Naranu kannin suru ga kannin*, enduring the unendurable is true endurance."

In this environment and with this role model, Yuki should have adopted a high sense of mission for Japan and the emperor. But he didn't. During his senior year Yuki struggled with doubts about transferring samurai ethics into national mission: *How do I know if Uncle Ken didn't use these values to justify colonization of Manchuria?* Yuki had deeper questions at the personal level: *How could I ever be a true samurai? Have I ever won a fight?*

13

I thought school was out. What are children doing in the courtyard? wondered Yuki as he passed the local Japanese school. Inside children stood in semicircles facing a *kamishibai* artist. *Kamishibai* (paper-play) is an inexpensive form of children's entertainment. The artist slides two-foot-square placards into a box, changing them as he narrates an action-packed story. After a performance the vendor sells small candies to entranced children. From childhood Yuki had witnessed *kamishibai* artists perform in Nagano. They had their own staccato-type delivery, using onomatopoeia and dialogue to keep children spellbound. The trade doesn't pay well; this is reflected in the shabby appearance of the artists.

Today's artist is different, arrestingly so. Tall, clean shaven, dressed in black trousers and white shirt, the artist appears to have nothing to sell. Yuki stopped to listen.

"Look at this gentleman from Jerusalem. He was a respected teacher. If he had lived in Tokyo, he would be a professor at Tokyo Imperial University. If he had lived in Changchun, he would be a teacher at Harbin University. He was not only a teacher, but a leader in government," said the vendor, sliding in the picture of a bearded man dressed in tunic and sandals. "He had so much knowledge and experience

Paper-play artist

that people came to him for advice. He was also very devout and carefully observed all the rules of his religion. But somehow he knew that wasn't enough. So one night, when no one could see him, he paid a visit to... ."

Yuki listened to the end. As the vendor was strapping the *kamishibai* box on his bicycle, Yuki asked, "Do you live in Changchun?"

"No. I'm on a summer mission from Japan. The church sent me here to work with children."

"How'd you get this far?" asked Yuki as he walked beside the artist pushing his cycle along.

"I caught a ship to Dairen and came here by train. Some private schools ask me to tell stories from Tolstoy, even the Bible."

"Being a Christian is considered disloyal these days. Aren't you afraid of Kwangtung police?

"Yes. I avoid them."

"You must have strong faith."

"No, I don't. In fact, I've taken this trip to strengthen my faith. Being a Christian isn't easy in Japan. I thought it might be easier in Manchuria. I was wrong."

I thought so, Yuki said to himself as he separated from the artist and turned down a path leading home. *Samurai became Christians during the Azuchi period (sixteenth century), but now it's unthinkable. No wonder the artist was having doubts.*

"Coming home, I saw a *kamishibai* artist performing at the primary school. It made me nostalgic for Nagano," reported Yuki to Uncle Ken. They were kneeling at a low table, using chopsticks for scooping up hot noodles from porcelain bowls. "He told a story about a teacher in Jerusalem, a teacher like you. I lost interest when he talked about faith, some kind of spirit, being born again. It made no sense."

"A Christian, I suppose?" asked Nakajima, as if he were trying to remember something.

"Yes. He was sent here by a Japanese church."

"I ran into an American Christian in Siberia back in 1919. He talked about a person he had never seen, that *Yaso* person. I admired the American, but... ."

"Couldn't follow his logic?" added Yuki, wanting to know his uncle's reaction.

"No, I couldn't. Remember in class I mentioned the Japanese approach to reality? The real is that which appears. We trust someone we see; those *Yaso* people trust someone they don't see."

"But faith, even weak faith, brought that artist all the way to Changchun."

"Now that you mention it, faith brought the American to Siberia. I wonder where he is now".

14

During Yuki's three years in Changchun, the boy with whom he shared his thoughts was a Chinese lad living in the same neighborhood. Yinhan Peng had recently come from Tokyo with his Taiwanese parents, newly appointed interpreters for Japanese bureaucrats in Changchun. Peng was tall for his age, big boned, having a large head with expressive face and inquisitive eyes. Quick to make friends, he lost them even quicker. His broad mind conceived grandiose plans, all to have them dashed by a short temper. More than once Yuki caught the full force of Peng's anger when the two disagreed. But Peng's anger lasted only a moment. Once understanding that, Yuki took Peng's outbursts in stride.

As the two grew closer, Peng felt free to discuss Japanese disdaining attitudes toward all Chinese, including himself.

"Do you feel that way?" asked Peng.

"Certainly not," replied Yuki, "Do you hate us Japanese?"

"No."

Whereupon the boys pledged loyalty to each other, swearing in solemn oaths never to let differences between Japan and China come between them. "If you are ever in any trouble I'll come help you," Yuki promised during their final time together. Peng, against his will, was being sent to Tokyo for higher education.

Yuki graduated from Changchun's Japanese high school in the Spring of 1936 and then retraced his steps to Dairen where a small steamer took him home. Ichiro and Fumiko warmly welcomed him at Niigata Harbor. Yuki soon learned that Japan, especially Nagano, was still in the grips of a crippling depression. College was out of the question, so he settled for part-time work between harvests. He was pleased to receive occasional letters from Peng.

"Yin," as Yuki called him, had been admitted to a prep school of Keio University, which all but assured college entrance.

In the summer of 1937, an envelope with official seals came from the local recruiting office. Yuki, now 20, had been conscripted for military service. After several months of basic training he entered the Medical Corpsman School and, completing that, was assigned to a unit destined for active duty overseas.

On October 22, 1937, Yuki lined up outside his barracks, then marched in formation to the train station for send-off speeches. The village headmaster began by reading excerpts from a recent government publication: "Our martial spirit does not have for its objective the killing of men, but the giving of life to men...it gives life to things through its strife. Here lies the martial spirit of our nation. War, in this sense, is not for the destruction, overpowering, or subjugation of others. It is for bringing about great harmony, that is, peace, doing the work of creation by following the Imperial Way."

While the speaker rambled on, Yuki's eyes ran down the line of recruits holding rifles aslant. Some had tucked family swords in their packs. *Giving life through strife?* Yuki was not the only one having difficulty with such reasoning; the crowd grew restless and began whispering. Another speaker tried paradox: "Cruel warlords have brought untold misery and hardships to the Chinese people. Our young men will end strife with strife." *End strife with strife*? Yuki wasn't sure.

Formalities over, a junior officer gave the command: "Shoulder arms! Right face! Forward March!" Ichiro and Fumiko waved flags as Yuki climbed aboard the waiting train. He threw open a window and poked his head out just as the crowd surged forward shouting, *"Banzai! Banzai!"* They were off.

Along a turbulent, silt-colored river that snaked down the mountain corridor to Nagoya, the train sped on through the afternoon. Yuki was moved to tears by so many people on station platforms waving red and white flags. From Nagoya the train moved slowly toward Osaka where, upon arrival, Yuki's unit

detrained and marched until dawn to the troop staging center where Yuki collapsed on his bedroll and slept through late morning. After several days of sightseeing in Osaka, the troops collected their gear and prepared for a final march to Tsukushi Harbor. There a rust-covered, sea-worn cargo vessel waited. It had been hastily refitted for troopship duty.

"What a miserable tub," blurted Yuki to a newly found friend, Corporal Tanaka, as they scrambled aboard in search of open space. At noon the following day the vessel left port and sailed along the Inland Sea with an eight-ship convoy bound for Nagasaki. As they left Bimon Straits, it began to drizzle. *Are these my parting tears?* thought a depressed Yuki. The ship rolling in heavy waves made him seasick.

Two more troopships lay waiting at anchor when Yuki's ship arrived off Goto Island near Nagasaki 24 hours later. That evening the company commander ordered all troops on deck. When they became silent, he explained their mission:

"Tomorrow we join the other troopships and head for Shanghai. We will be escorted by the battle cruiser you see across the bay. Once in Shanghai we will disembark and become part of a seventy-thousand force attacking Chinese forces between Shanghai and Nanking. General Matsui Iwane will lead the assault against warlord Tang, who is defending the southern capital. Already five Japanese divisions are assembled."

Most of the men, including Yuki, spent their last night in Japan on deck enjoying *sake*, listening to Victrola music, and sharing stories of home. The following day at 7:00 a.m. the convoy sailed westerly and by noon entered the East China Sea. High waves battering Yuki's ship brought wrenching seasickness, made worse by sheets of chill rain that kept troops confined below decks. After two days the sea turned muddy in color; landfall was imminent and the captain ordered a total blackout.

15

When the troops ventured out on deck next morning, Japanese aircraft flying overhead, navy ships moving in and out of the Shanghai estuary lifted their spirits. Word came that the clogged harbor could not handle all the infantry at once; medical corpsman would leave first to aid scurvy-ridden troops. With packs slung over their shoulders, Yuki's unit stepped ashore and followed a junior officer who seemed to know where he was going. They marched inland 5 kilometers to Kinzan, a suburb of Shanghai, where they would bivouac for the night. Along the way Yuki observed enormous battle emplacements with corpses strewn everywhere, evidently left by fleeing Chinese artillery units. Yuki stepped over to look at one body, a youth in padded jacket and green leggings. There he lay face up, no shoes, skin the color of parchment. Yuki noticed the pale shine of eye white from his large head, covered with coarse-textured black hair. Yuki paused. The youth bore a resemblance to Yinhan Peng. Changchun memories charged into his mind, almost a diversion from the present horror. *I hope Yin understands we're doing this for China's good. Peace will not come until the people are delivered from warlords like Tang.*

At Kinzan they made a blazing campfire to cut the cold and cook huge pots of rice. Prospects for needed sleep grew dim when rain began to fall with no sign of stopping, so they gathered up their gear and slogged on through the night along paths churned into muddy slime. Stormy weather slowed their pace, as did merely trying to live in a new environment. Days at sea with poor food and little exercise had not prepared them for this. It took hours just to cook, eat, and take naps. When would they make it to the front lines? After marching 4 kilometers they stopped at a bomb-damaged house, took off rain-soaked packs, and lit another fire. Smoke rose to the ceiling and hovered over shivering neophytes hoping against hope their officer would call a halt. He did, and posted a guard so the men could sleep until dawn.

By 4:00 a.m. they were off again toward the Front, their path taking form as hints of daylight broke through the mist. By 8:00 a.m. they reached Shinsochin, a rail junction where Japanese troops had spread artillery field pieces along a line and were firing at Chinese positions. *We made it!* thought Yuki, removing his pack near a field kitchen, only to be startled by a roar in the distance.

"What's that noise?"

"Answers from our thankful hosts," quipped Tanaka. "You know, the ones we've come to save."

Just then another corpsman rushed up, out of breath: "I just learned from the command post that A company has come under heavy fire at Kairikyo. They need medical corpsmen. We're to join auxiliary units sent to relieve them. We leave this afternoon. Let's get some food down first. "

All the field cooks could provide was stale, long-grain Chinese rice without *miso* soup or vegetables. "Tastes awful," Yuki mumbled between his chopsticks. At 4:00 p.m. the three corpsmen fell behind the assigned auxiliary unit and headed out toward Kairikyo.

By then the Chinese countryside had become

familiar. It looked like a deserted piece of flat land—neglected fields, shelled farmhouses standing on stilt-like pillars blackened by fire, drainage ditches filled with brackish water and debris. *The work of warlords? Couldn't be... Who then?* pondered Yuki.

Chinese defenders evidently got wind of a Japanese relief column headed for Kairikyo. When the new moon silhouetted Yuki's unit against an abandoned farmhouse, snipers opened fire. Yuki leaped into an open ditch, but Tanaka kept moving against another

fusillade that swept across the field. Yuki saw several men fall. Through the dust and confusion a searchlight probed for moving forms. When the blinding light passed Yuki, he knew his moment had come. Over the ditch he leaped and raced for the fallen men. *Tanaka! Not you!* He bent close to check Tanaka's vital signs. *Ah, still breathing!* Next he cut away the reddened area of the shirt. *In the shoulder! Above his heart!* Yuki then tore off cotton swaths to staunch the bleeding. *Here comes the searchlight!* He held Tanaka tightly and feigned death. When the searchlight moved on, Yuki threw down his pack and positioned himself under Tanaka's limp body. With one stupendous effort he stumbled forward, Tanaka piggyback, pack in hand, and made for the ditch. Within minutes relief units caught up with them. Yuki pressed two men into getting Tanaka back to the First Aid Tent at Shinsochin. As medics examined Tanaka, Yuki collapsed on a cot nearby. *Why so exhausted? Hello! What's this? On my arm? Blood oozing from hair follicles?* He grabbed a small mirror from his pack and looked again, rolling up pant legs. *Not only from arms but legs.* He opened his mouth and stared. *Sure enough, gums are red and sore. Scurvy!*

Auxiliary units around Kairikyo were checked by the dogged defenders and could advance no further toward Nanking. As medic-in-charge Yuki was ordered to accompany the severely wounded, including Tanaka, back to Shanghai and home to Japan. In Osaka, a medical checkup determined that because of scurvy Yuki should be deactivated. It appeared that his war days were over. The growing appetite of the military meant he could serve his country just as well farming. Yuki went on inactive reserve status, returned to Nagano, and began assisting his father in rice cultivation.

Later Yuki learned about General Matsui Iwane and his troops as they advanced toward Nanking in December of 1937. General Tang's soldiers scattered before them in a pell-mell rout that swelled to maniacal panic as the fighting neared the gates of Nanking. A report of what ensued—the Rape of Nanking—came from Japan's Foreign Minister Hirota Koki after his inspection trip in January 1938: "The Japanese army behaved in a fashion reminiscent of Attila and his Huns." Yuki knew something had gone tragically wrong.

16

Yuki had turned 24, was in good health again, and could be recalled any time. If something were to happen to him, an only son, the Nakajima line would be cut off. His father, Ichiro, sent out feelers to village families with girls of marriageable age. After auspicious cosmic phenomena were divined and family trees traced on both sides, the choice narrowed down to one girl. In April Yuki married Kazuko, demure, nurtured by village life, schooled in the samurai tradition. She exemplified the

Japanese character for wife (*woman-holding-broom*). Uncle Ken would approve.

Times were unsettling for everyone except farmers. War clouds were gathering in the western Pacific; Japan must strengthen defense lines along borders of empire and increase home food production. Supply lines from colonies like Manchuria or Taiwan could be cut any time. At government insistence farm co-ops were forming to insure prioritized military distribution, a prelude to rice rationing. The young couple could sell all the rice they could produce, and at a good price.

In June, before monsoon rains make it difficult, they transplant hand-nurtured rice shoots from small paddies to large. Today, Yuki and Kazuko stand ankle-deep in muddy water, shielded from the sun by cloud cover. Both are dressed in dark-blue *mompei*, coveralls, and shod in split-toed, sock-like canvas shoes. With rapid movement they thrust down handfuls of young rice shoots into wet soil.

At the end of one paddy Yuki pauses to wipe his forehead, then faces Kazuko. "Yesterday, the co-op director gave me some disturbing news."

"What's that?" asked Kazuko, visibly shaken.

"Because of manpower shortages overseas, older men of the village may be drafted and those on medical leave reactivated."

Splash! Into the water from Kazuko's hand falls a clump of mud with rice shoots. Her eyes rivet his. "But I'm pregnant. They keep talking about the nation as a family. This is a cruel joke. Tojo's war-faction is tearing our family apart. Master-and-servant is only one of the five Confucian relationships. What about the others? Like husband-and-wife. Or father-and-son? Are these not to be honored? How can one relationship cancel the other two? Can't you refuse? For my sake? You yourself say the Chinese don't want us."

"Kazuko. Listen to me. Some force, a force we can't see, touch, or explain makes our leaders do irrational things. There is no way they can defeat China. We must fight against that force, whatever it is, and I can't do that from a deserters' prison," pleaded Yuki, holding his wife's weeping face.

Two days later an envelope with red seals came from the local army recruiting office. Yuki had been ordered back to active duty. After several months of advanced training, Yuki was assigned to the 73rd Eastern Battalion, about to be deployed overseas. On September 12, 1941, the 73rd embarked on a troopship bound for Manchuria and reached Dairen four days later. From there they were sent on guard duty to Sekimonshi, a station on the Manchuria-Russian border. Yuki's unit swung into action, digging wells, erecting field tents, and carrying out military maneuvers. Their routine was broken by a long overdue military packet from home, in which were undelivered cables. Yuki opened Kazuko's: "Baby boy safely delivered February 15th. Hurry home."

Men of the 73rd were not prepared for extreme cold temperatures, but, making the best of a bad situation, removed rock from a convex area, poured in water, and created a skating rink. Makeshift barracks were no defense against icy winds. Wolves bayed at night. When he would flash his light into the forest, Yuki could make out pairs of eyes in the distance, mere pinpricks of light, roaming back and forth. All was not hostile, however. Local Chinese youth volunteers produced lettuce and potatoes for the Japanese garrison. It appeared that the 73rd would be stationed there indefinitely. But Japan's advance down the Malay Peninsula and invasion of East Java changed all that.

In early March 1942, the 73rd left Sekimonshi and at Dairen boarded a troopship for Taiwan where, upon arrival, it joined a large task force bound for Hong Kong. There more troopships were waiting, and together a 40-ship convoy sailed from Hong Kong, ostensibly to support imperial land forces moving south along the Malay Peninsula. Unable to enter Singapore's harbor, part of the convoy, including Yuki's troopship, diverted further south toward the Dutch East Indies and entered Merauke Bay at dusk on March 22nd.

Storming the beach had already begun. Yuki saw bursts of light from shore batteries followed by plumes of water near Japanese units as they waded ashore from lead transports. *Dutch defenders evidently knew we were coming. Who told them?* Just then several Japanese battle cruisers entered the bay and opened fire on British destroyers maneuvering to launch torpedoes. One was hit. Huge flames shot into the air. Under cover of darkness Yuki's troopship moved cautiously toward the harbor but, while evading torpedoes, struck another Japanese ship, listed to port, and began to roll over on its side. Most of the troops, however, slid down the wet hull and then pushed off into waist-high water, holding packs overhead. Yuki was with them.

A force this size overwhelmed Java troops; hundreds were captured. Hardly had Yuki made it ashore when he was ordered to set up a first-aid station. Life became hectic, living not from day to day but minute to minute, and that under conflicting commands. For example, to traverse shallow rivers the construction battalion made a human bridge by laying wooden planks on shoulders of infantry troops. Yuki was pressed into this duty.

After two weeks, the 73rd moved inland, leaving Yuki behind with the sick and wounded. He was not prepared for the oppressive climate. Moisture filled the air. It dripped from the trees like sap, it made distant hills quiver in the sunlight, and it invaded clothing until Yuki's shirt clung to him like a wet rag. People walked slowly, wild goats stood motionless in the grass, and monkeys gaped down from trees like fixtures. At night scorpions crawled into Yuki's tent and down his boots.

Yet there were lighter moments. After getting accustomed to their invaders, Javanese youth played baseball with the troops. One afternoon Yuki sat down to watch the fun. A Javanese sitting nearby caught his attention; he seemed to be Chinese. To test his hunch Yuki greeted him in Chinese. Stunned, the youth replied,

"Do you speak Chinese?"

"A little," said Yuki, standing up. He pointed to a spot away from the others and beckoned the youth to follow. They squatted on the damp grass, folded their legs, and kept their eyes focused on the game. The Javanese youth continued,

"Where did you learn Chinese?

"In North China… I attended a Japanese high school there. And you?"

"My parents immigrated here from Fukien province. I'm native born."

"How do you stand this humidity? In the worst of summer Japan is never like this. Even if I could play baseball, only a fool would run around those bases. What makes it so hot?"

"We're only 10 degrees from the equator. You get used to it. I feel it most during rice harvest."

"You're farmers?"

"Well, we were until the invasion. My family fled to the hills."

"They didn't need to. We've come to liberate you from the Dutch."

"Liberate? From the Dutch? Everything we have we owe to them. Steady income from crops. Schools. Hospitals. Churches."

"Churches?"

"Yes. My parents became Christians here. So have most ethnic Chinese."

"Maybe we're here for the oil," admitted Yuki.

"Oil? Why doesn't Japan pay for it like everyone else?"

"We're willing but can't. The Allied embargo turned off our biggest oil tap in the Pacific. We're here to turn it back on."

"It won't be easy. Retreating Dutch soldiers have clogged the wells, and last week one of our fishermen reported a large submarine offshore. It may be American."

Yuki didn't want to hear more and stood up. He held out his hand as if to help the ethnic Chinese, who sprang to his feet and stepped out of arm's reach, as if to say, "No thank you!" Yuki never saw him again.

17

Japanese forces continued to mop up sporadic resistance throughout the Dutch East Indies. Meanwhile, a naval battle that would alter the course of the war loomed in the western Pacific. It began when a Japanese armada advanced toward the mid-Pacific to annihilate remnants of the United States Pacific Fleet and secure a vital outpost—the island of Midway. Unknown to Japanese commanders, the U.S. had broken the Japanese code. This enabled American carriers to pinpoint the Japanese naval force and on June 4th, 1942, sink four carriers—the *Akagi*, *Kaga*, *Hiryu*, and *Soryu*.

This strategic loss left Japan without mobile air power to cover operations in the south Pacific; in particular, to protect ground troops in the Solomon Islands. US Marines had already overrun Henderson Field at Guadalcanal. To retake the airfield, Japan launched fierce land, sea, and air battles. On August 8, the Battle of Solomon Islands. On August 23-24, the Second Battle of the Solomon Islands. On the nights of October 11-12, the Esperansa Cape Sea battle. On October 26-27, the Battle of Santa Cruz.

Though Yuki knew little about those battles, he sensed something had gone wrong. For one thing, he didn't see many tankers in port siphoning off oil reserves. Army units began digging in, camouflaging gun emplacements with foliage. For all practical purposes, Japan had ceased being an offensive force in the Pacific. Her military endeavors turned defensive; she could only hope to fight a war of attrition until Allied powers grew weary and sued for peace.

In October 1942, the 73rd was reassigned to Sekimonshi in Manchuria. While his troopship went through Malaysian waters, Yuki contracted malaria but refused treatment at a field hospital ashore, fearing separation from the 73rd. It was a good decision. By the time the ship reached Dairen, Yuki's malaria had subsided. Again his unit was assigned patrol duty on the increasingly volatile Chinese-Russian border. After two years he came up for promotion. It was then that a review of Yuki's bravery under fire near Nanking and steady head in battle netted him an appointment to officer training.

He arrived in Toyohashi, Shizuoka Prefecture, in December 1944 and entered the army cadet school. There he made friends with another officer-cadet,

Adachi, a graduate of Tokyo University. In the barracks Yuki shared with Adachi his misgivings about Japan's expansionism and subjugation of Asian neighbors. Adachi had similar reservations. He, too, had been caught in the vortex of Japan's all-the-world-under-one-roof jingoism before realizing its sober implications, not only militarily but culturally.

"At Yamagata High school we were given military training," recounted Adachi. "It involved forced marches to the local Gokoku Temple. There we were required to bow and pay respects to Japan's war dead. My family was Christian. For me, enforced Shinto worship uncovered the darker side of militarism. It became darker still when the government suppressed contrary ideologies such as democracy, pacifism, and individual freedom."

"I was taught Bushido by my uncle in Manchuria but later saw its outworking with our troops on the way to Nanking," said Yuki, feeling a kindred spirit with Adachi. "I'm sure you know what General Matsui's troops did there. I didn't enter the city, but heard what happened. Nanking made me question our whole China involvement."

"I remember," added Adachi, "as a seventh grader going on parades to send off troops from Yamagata, shouting '*Banzai!*' Then, toward the end of high school, when those same young men returned home as cremated bones wrapped in white linen, I began having doubts."

"Why, then, did you join up?" queried Yuki.

"I was drafted. Officer quotas were filled by reducing university courses to two and a half years. I graduated early in December of 1941 but was not called up immediately. Instead, I took employment with *Mitsubishi Kasei*, a large chemical subsidiary of the *Mitsubishi* conglomerate. As you remember, at first the war went well for Japan. No one would have guessed my doubts, the way I joined others on night parades, holding lanterns to celebrate Japan's victories. By August of 1942 my time for military service had come. I was conscripted as a private, but later applied for officer training. They sent me here in Spring, 1944."

Several days later, in their social-history class, an officer instructor encouraged cadets to express their opinions about the war. "Speak candidly," he said. At that time anti-war sentiment was taboo. Moreover, it was politically correct to call the Pacific War a "holy war." So, most cadets answered accordingly. Adachi, however, spoke his mind: "In any war, men kill each other. Thus I believe war is the greatest of all evils." Walking out of class together, Yuki said, "Now you won't pass the final interview before commissioning."

Contrary to Yuki's prediction, Adachi finished at the head of the class, and this landed him a teaching post with the Air Force in Osaka. Yuki was not so lucky. In January 1945, he was sent to defend the most fiercely contested island of the Pacific War—Okinawa.

18

The American landing on Okinawa, April 1, 1945, was no surprise to dug-in Japanese defenders. It was the next logical step for the Allies, halving the distance for B-29s bombing Japan from the Marianas. The Allied armada included more than 40 aircraft carriers, 18 battleships, 200 destroyers, and 430 troop ships carrying more than 3 marine and 4 army divisions. Twenty-five vessels carried nothing but Jeeps. In command was Lt. General Simon Bolivar Buckner, son of a Civil War general.

At first the Americans met no resistance. General Mitsuru Ushijima had withdrawn his men to man-made tunnels extending for miles under the southern end of the 60-mile island. The men waited underground. It was a honeycombed defense combining tunnels, old castles, and mini-forts. Yuki and his platoon huddled together with food supplies, water, rifles, and ammunition in a natural cave.

Shell hole by shell hole, cave by cave, the Americans kept coming, prying Japanese troops from underground. Flame-throwers were the weapon of choice, accounting for a quarter of the one hundred and seven thousand soldiers killed. When Yuki saw licks of flame jabbing into the cave's mouth, he felt his cartridge belt. Before death, it is said the mind becomes lucid: Yuki remembered a samurai incident from one of Uncle Ken's lectures. Nearly a century before, southern samurai in the name of the emperor wanted to fight Western "barbarians" to the bitter end. Northern samurai knew better. They sued for peace. One even slipped away to Yokohama, traded his suicide knife for an English dictionary, and sought out the barbarians.

The flames were getting closer. Before his astonished troops Yuki pulled from his cartridge belt not more bullets but a carefully concealed thin white towel.

"Stop!" they yelled, jumping between him and the cave entrance. Yuki froze before fixing his eyes on their smudged faces. He spoke with a boldness that surprised even him: "I order you to stand aside!

In minutes, you'll be incinerated. What can your ashes do for Japan? Enduring the unendurable is true endurance!"

Yuki walked straight toward the man-made barricade as if it didn't exist. The master sergeant looked down and then stepped aside. Others did likewise. Yuki rushed to the mouth of the cave, tied the towel around his bayonet and waved it back and forth. Flames curled away from the entrance, then died. All was silent. Out walked Yuki with hands up, followed by his terrified men. For them the war was over.

19

A rusted gray Landing Ship Tank (LST) from Okinawa nears a pier at the Sasebo naval base in southwestern Japan. Formerly the ship beached and disgorged tanks from steel doors. Today those doors are sealed watertight, and in the bays are not tanks but Japanese soldiers about to be repatriated to the homeland. With gear in readiness they sit on cots spread over the deck. To the port side is a galley where men line up for their last meal.

Yuki stood close to the bow, watching the approach. No friends or family in sight. The only greeters were US Military Police who would escort troops to Central Station for the trip home.

With lifted spirit and trusted pack, Yuki disembarked. At the bottom of the gangplank, each man showed his identification to a waiting MP and his Japanese interpreter. When Yuki presented his, the interpreter showed surprise. *"Chotto matte!* Just a minute!" The MP vanished then returned, pointing to the side, "Stand over there. You will not be going home directly." The Supreme Command of Allied Powers (SCAP) had issued a directive to detain Okinawa officers. MPs will accompany Yuki to Tokyo.

Upon reaching Sugamo prison in greater Tokyo, Yuki was told his fate: he is among the 5,700 military and civilian personnel to stand trial before the Allied War Crimes Tribunal in early 1946.

The goal of the tribunal was to establish moral responsibility for crimes against the peace and crimes against humanity. The tribunal also set out to discover ideological factors condoning such crimes. In the eyes of Allied prosecutors, dismissing Japanese behavior as the logical outcome of ultra-nationalism begged the question. Every nation state is undergirded by the national consciousness of its people. In the nineteenth century this consciousness expressed itself in colonialism. But, to the Japanese elite there was a qualitative difference between western colonialism motivated by economic interests or "the white man's burden," and Japan's expansionism. The latter, being the will of the emperor, was considered a moral act. By its nature, national polity was unable to do wrong. Accordingly, the most atrocious behavior, the most treacherous acts, could all be condoned. Such attitudes emerged during those trials in Tokyo.

Each day Yuki sat to the rear with other officers. It was a solemn scene—black-robed jurors, representing every country of the Allies, sitting to the left; Japan's elite of the military clique, seated directly in front of the prosecutor's podium; junior officers like Yuki, to the rear; reporters and journalists, to the right; tan-shirted MPs with billy clubs, standing on the perimeter.

Through a brilliant interpreter for the accused Yuki heard long indictments ranging from mass murder of civilian populations to ill-treatment of prisoners, verified by 449 first-hand witnesses. This included sword-brandishing officers on horseback going down the line of the infamous Bataan Death March, hacking to death American prisoners who fell out of line through sheer exhaustion and dehydration. Tying live Allied prisoners to stakes for bayonet and rifle practice. Hydrax-gassing Chinese civilian populations. Killing and raping nearly 100,000 Philippine civilians as General Homma's troops fled Manila. Performing medical experiments without anesthesia on Manchurian prisoners. Beheading tattooed Shanghai youth on suspicion they were members of Secret Societies.

Removing his glasses and facing the stunned audience and black-robed jurors from eleven victim nations, prosecutor Keenan concluded:

"These were not isolated excesses of undisciplined troops gone berserk. From top to bottom the Japanese military had been imbued with an ethic that considered prisoners of war subhuman, specimens for experiment. The elite sitting in the dock before you were proximate the emperor. Nothing else was needed. No international law, no Geneva Convention restrained them. Prisoners were distant from the emperor, so distant they could not qualify for human sympathy. In contrast to a 4 percent war-prisoner death rate in German POW camps, Japanese camps had a whopping 27 percent."

These allegations were shocking enough, but to Yuki their defense went beyond belief. Keenan continued, "Perpetrators in the Philippine camps did not kick and beat prisoners in cold blood. Such actions were for the good of the camp." Kwantung Army colonels in Manchuria were not restrained by an inner law condemning murder of innocent civilians. Rather, duty on behalf of the Emperor made their acts moral. Answers by the defendants made this abundantly clear. In their minds morality was neither an abstract consciousness of legality nor an internal sense of right and wrong, nor a concept of serving the public. It was a feeling of being close to the concrete entity known as the Emperor, an entity that could be directly perceived by the senses. It was therefore only natural that these high-ranking officers should come to identify their own interests with those of the Emperor.

Yuki leaned forward to hear how General Minami handled challenges to this flawed assumption.

Q: President of the Court: "Why did you call it a 'Holy War?'"

A: General Minami: "I used the word because it was in wide currency at the time."

Q: "What was holy about it?"

A: "I never thought about it very deeply. I just happened to use the word because it was used at that time among the general public. My idea was that this was not an aggressive war but one that had arisen owing to unavoidable circumstances."

When the prosecutor questioned Foreign Minister Togo about his personal reservations in contrast to his public support of the Tripartite Pact with Germany and Italy, Togo replied, "Well, there was no latitude in public speeches to include my personal likes or dislikes...It would be more accurate to say that as Foreign Minister of Japan, I was in such a position that I had to make speeches of that nature, rather than to say there was no room for truth."

Yuki wondered how Admiral Koiso would respond to the prosecutor's logic: "You, Admiral Koiso, say you tried to prevent the Manchurian Incident. You opposed the Tripartite Pact. You opposed going to war with the United States. You tried to settle the China War when you became premier. In all of these important matters you were frustrated and prevented from having your ideas and desires prevail. Why then did you accept one important government position after another whereby you became one of the protagonists of the very matters to which you now say you strenuously objected?"

Koiso looked up, then down, but finally muttered, "The way of us Japanese is that no matter what our personal opinions and our own personal arguments may be, once a policy of State has been decided upon, it is our duty to bend all our efforts for the prosecution of such policy. This has been the traditional custom in our country."

Yuki couldn't believe his ears. Koiso was the State, a principal drafter of war policy, but in his defense uses passive verbs, as if someone or something else decides policy. *Does this mean the Japanese state is governed by blind circumstance? Fate? Inevitability? Surely Koiso knows blind forces did not plunge Japan into the abyss.* Koiso's obfuscation revealed how nearness to the Emperor, the human embodiment of moral value, enabled Bushido mentality to silence promptings of conscience. *"I've been evil's accomplice,* thought Yuki, slumping down in his chair.

At the end, out of the total 5,700 indicted by the tribunal, over 3,000 were convicted and 900 executed. Against Yuki, however, no specific offense could be cited. Cleared of all charges in June 1946, he was issued a return ticket to Matsumoto City in Nagano, and ushered to the gate of the Sugamo prison barracks. The gate opened and closed. For the last time he put his arms through the straps of the tattered pack and walked toward Sugamo station. Passers-by glanced at his faded army uniform and then looked away. From Sugamo he went to Shinjuku station and lined up for the evening train to Matsumoto City. After sitting for hours on newspapers spread on the concrete platform, Yuki slowly rose to his feet and climbed aboard the waiting train. All seats were taken. He would have to stand in the aisle, a conspicuous symbol of Japan's greatest tragedy. Fortunately, a worse symbol appeared, as the train picked up momentum. Yuki heard chords from a broken accordion playing what sounded like a funeral dirge but was really *Kimigayo*, the national anthem. The player, dressed in soiled white clothes, bowed to the passengers, said something Yuki couldn't hear, and then moved down the aisle with an offering box dangling from an arm stump. *Ah, another veteran! At least I have all my limbs and a family who cares.*

His parents stood in the Matsumoto station with Kazuko at their side. In farm clothing as threadbare as his own, Ichiro and Fumiko looked up at Yuki from a bent-over position. Neither could stand erect. *They've had to do all the rice planting without me,* thought Yuki. *Even Kazuko has aged. So young, yet lines are etched around her eyes and lips.* They reached out to take Yuki's pack, but he grabbed it away. Mounting the waiting rickshaw, Yuki's thoughts went back to the day he left Nagano for Manchuria. He must somehow muster up the same stoic determination that sent him away 14 years ago.

The old samurai spirit could not be revived. Disillusioned, Yuki withdrew to a Buddhist temple, seeking answers through Zen austerities, but to no avail. He had lost all purpose in life, all reason for living. When offered command of a self-defense unit, Yuki refused. No state-sponsored organization could be trusted. He determined to go through the chaotic post-war period depending only on himself. After finding employment with *Mitsubishi Foods* through retired Uncle Ken, Yuki settled down in Nagaoka city in Niigata prefecture. His lasting achievement for Japan would be raising a new generation of sons devoted to family, not country.

20

Ensign Matt Kingsbury, Jr had his 20th birthday aboard the *USS Leonard Wood* bound for Japan. The Navy supply ship had been named after an officer in the 1918 American Expeditionary Force to Siberia. Mid-Pacific, while standing on deck, Matt Jr saw something in the water 30 yards to starboard. *Whoa! What's that? A huge ball! Covered with rust! Spikes all over!*

The captain, furious because the mine went undetected, circled back to detonate it with anti-aircraft guns. The explosion sent plumes of water upward and shrapnel everywhere. Matt ducked under a gun tub. He was a passenger under orders to another ship—*Destroyer 699*—in Yokosuka. Several days before landfall, on the port side of the *Leonard Wood* an American destroyer squadron was sighted heading east. With binoculars Matt tried to make out numerals on each bow. *Of all things*! he gasped. One was *699* heading east while Matt headed west. Now what would the Navy do with him?

As Matt's ship pulled into Yokosuka Bay he noticed the damaged battleship *Nagato* at anchor. It stood out among other Japanese warships anchored nearby. Having no destroyer to join, Matt was ordered with other officers to board a Japanese light-cruiser still manned by Japanese personnel. They were to prepare the cruiser for its final journey—to Eniwetok Atoll in the Western Pacific. There it would suffer the fate of other war-booty ships: destruction by a subsurface atomic blast. Two things about the cruiser caught Matt's attention: flimsy hatch handles (*could they control flooding*?) and barrels of dried grasshoppers in the ship's galley (*do sailors really eat them*?). One friendly Japanese officer ushered Matt to his stateroom and produced a small photo album highlighting his naval career. As torpedo officer he had damaged an American aircraft carrier in the Battle of the Philippine Sea. The last picture showed him in a lifeboat wearing a life-preserver. His command returned him to Japan where he was reassigned to this ship as the war ended.

Since only six months remained in Matt's term of naval service, he was given opportunity to leave the Japanese cruiser before it set sail for Eniwetok. The Navy command then assigned him to the destroyer-tender *Piedmont*, tied up at a Yokosuka pier, serving other ships that came alongside for repair. The day after Matt took over the ship's 1st division, a sailor was tragically killed. He had tripped over a hatch and fell to the bottom compartment. Matt collected his personal effects and sent his sea bag with a condolence letter to the next of kin.

It was an inauspicious beginning. Men of the 1st division were a seasoned lot. They had been in the western Pacific over two years. In the Philippines, a ship anchored alongside the *Piedmont* had mysteriously exploded, inflicting casualties on both ships. Now in Japan, the ship's crew was enjoying a well-earned respite. On to this scene walked Matt, a young ensign with no sea or war experience. One hundred and twenty men standing in formation on the forecastle deck eyed their new commander. By the muffled laughter Matt knew their thoughts: *Younger than all of us. Does he know anything?* Sure enough, men began neglecting routine chores. After the 1st division failed to pass captain's inspection, Matt tried to remedy the situation. This involved hauling a derelict bo'suns mate before the executive officer and challenging the most defiant sailor to a boxing match at the base gym.

Matt's foremost collateral duty sent him on shore patrol. Reports of US servicemen abusing Japanese civilians were becoming all too frequent. In response, MacArthur ordered shore patrols to nearby towns where robberies had been reported. With a Shore Patrol band strapped around his arm Matt stood alone at his assigned station, making sure sailors didn't get off trains. Since few made the attempt, Matt had time on his hands. A small toy-like trolley rolled to a stop and opened its doors. Japanese men clambered aboard, leaving women and children behind. *How about a lesson in Western chivalry?* Before the next trolley pulled up, Matt formed two lines— one for women and children, the other for men.

When the trolley door opened, he motioned for women and children to board, while blocking the men's line. Passengers dutifully boarded as directed. No one questioned this cultural intrusion.

21

In a large jeep Matt drove several sailors over potholed roads to an auditorium in Hibiya Park, Tokyo. The unheated hall, suffering from war neglect, made music appreciation difficult at best. Matt walked in with the sailors and moved down the aisle looking for empty seats. Before them stood Japanese collegians and American servicemen, holding choral sheets about to sing "The Hallelujah Chorus." Matt couldn't believe what he was seeing and hearing—erstwhile enemies lifting voices in praise. The final words, "And He shall reign forever and ever" reverberated through his mind as the symphony ended.

In contrast, upon leaving the hall, Matt was overwhelmed by the tragic aftermath of man's misrule. Scenes of desolation and devastation rushed by as the jeep sped back to the *Piedmont*, passing mile after mile of bombed-out residential districts. The only lights were those flickering from wood fires where families stood warming themselves. *I don't see how they keep warm.* The same scenes raced by again and again: Japanese with packs on their backs, trudging on, no telling where; wooden-wheeled carts filled with firewood or scrap metal or vats of human excrement for fertilizer. All this in the dead of night. Matt was chilled to the bone when he got to the ship and took a steaming shower to thaw out.

By now Matt had settled into a daily routine

aboard the *Piedmont*. Ship duties were punctuated by occasional trips to the surrounding countryside with men of the 1st Division. In mid-March he journeyed with a truckload of off-duty sailors to the Hakone resort area. Around the curves near

Miyanoshita, as the truck slowed down, men jumped out the back and vanished. His would-be charges gone, Matt sent the truck back empty and took in the scenery, beginning with a rowboat ride on Lake Ashinoko. Along the shoreline a red Shinto shrine came into view. *What happens at these shrines?* Leaving the boat, Matt walked up to the red-pillared entrance with horizontal beam overhead. Just then a line of priests entered, prostrated themselves on the shrine floor, and chanted something. *Were they praying? To whom?*

By dusk Matt was aboard a crowded, smoke-filled train swaying down the mountain. Most men in the coach were dressed in drab, threadbare army uniform. Jammed against him in the aisle stood three middle-school children in dark-blue school outfits, chatting away. He compared them with Americans having plenty to eat, warm homes and bright futures. *What is before these children? How must God view them? Of course, with love. If so, why don't you?* He prayed, *Lord, I will love them.* Instantly warm feelings toward the Japanese poured over him. Just then the train doors opened. The children were gone.

Upon return to the ship Matt learned that men from the ship's chapel had been invited to a Friday night youth meeting at the Kamakura Methodist church. He joined them. The pastor, having studied in America, volunteered to interpret for the sailors who sang and shared their faith. The meeting concluded, but for some reason the Japanese young people lingered. They had something to say. One looked up, obviously troubled. She had written out her thoughts: "Why does God permit such evil in the world?" and "I do not want salvation from a God who permits little babies to suffer and die because of their parents." Another, with tears in her eyes, looked up at Matt and pleaded, "When you return to your people and see the Chinese and Philippine people, will you tell them I am sorry for what our military has done?"

One Japanese youth, Muramatsu, was particularly responsive and could speak broken English.

"Could I visit your home?" asked Matt.

"I alone with mother. Small house on hill. No heat. You okay?"

"Of course."

Muramatsu led Matt and another sailor up a small knoll near the Zushi station. The modest house where he lived with his mother was barren and cold. Windows were open. No electric lights. Before stepping up on the mat floor, the sailors removed shoes but kept on overcoats. Flickering candles silhouetted their bent figures against rice-papered panels. As they curled numb fingers around a coal brazier, Muramatsu explained their greatest loss of the war:

"B-29 fire bombs hit Yokohama house. Kill father. With mother run here to mountain. I still sad."

Matt tried to offer some word of hope, "Let us pray that God our Heavenly Father will take care of you." He wasn't exactly sure how all this would work out. In fact those comforting words to Matsumura discomfited Matt. *What are you talking about? Would you trade places with Muramatsu? Let him return to the ship. You remain here. You face his future, with the message you just gave him. Are you willing? No. Then, why are you talking this way?* Muramatsu had no idea he was listening to a doubting Thomas. The three of them made their way down the hill, singing hymns as they went. In the Zushi train tunnel, they prayed again and exchanged farewells.

In early January 1946, dock men threw off thick hawsers from the Yokosuka pier as the *Piedmont* edged away. Sailors and officers lined the ship's rail. Matt stood on deck with men from the ship's chapel, gazing at a small hill overlooking the dock. There, thin figures stood waving white flags; youth from the Kamakura church had come as promised. *Will I ever see them again? Or Japan?* Such thoughts crossed Matt's mind as he took his station on the bridge.

22

The freighter J. L. Luckenbach plowed through heavy waves and high winds. Matt Jr and his family hadn't expected cruise weather along the Great Circle route to Japan. Even so, they were unprepared for the great winds and wild waves battering the ship. They were soon forbidden to go on deck at all. Tons of steel I-beams, destined for the U.S. military in occupied Japan, were crashing alternately between the hatch and ship rails. The ship, pitching in 40-foot waves, gave force to their movement, causing them to break restraining cables and bend rails outward, over the water. The hatch was struck next, as the ship rolled in the opposite direction.

Vigils at the porthole became an obsession. The children were afraid to watch and afraid not to watch. Perched atop moving mountains of water, the ship shuddered. Dishes crashed to the galley floor. Books tumbled from the cabin dresser. But all was insignificant compared to the action on the deck beneath their porthole. Between rolls, deckhands tried to regain control and replace snapped cables. It wasn't until the I-beams were safely restrained hours later that the officers said they held dangerous potential. Had they broken every chain and slid over the side, the ship would have listed precariously. As they fell, given full force by the crashing waves, they could have damaged the ship's hull.

The ship's crew found the young family ready targets for humor, warning them to eat well in preparation for the future: "It'll be fish heads and rice as soon as you get off this ship," they taunted. Matt's wife, Elaine, didn't know whether to believe them or not; this was her first venture abroad. She stood a foot shorter than Matt, with a trim figure, dark-brown hair.

Soon after Japan's surrender and occupation by Allied forces, General Douglas MacArthur sent out a call for missionaries. The pervasive sense of meaninglessness that followed Japan's defeat had created a spiritual vacuum. Matt Jr and Elaine were among the two thousand who responded to this call. They joined a small Mission working in north-central Japan. One month before their departure, Matt Jr's father sent a probing letter to the only person he knew in Japan—Ken Nakajima, retired and living in Nagaoka. The letter read:

"I don't know if this will reach you or not. My son and his family leave for Japan next month, in response to MacArthur's call for missionaries. While showing them memorabilia from my time in Siberia, we came across your Nagano address, written in our wedding book. Matt will be with a small English Mission working in north-central Japan. Are you far from Gumma? Matt Jr and his wife Elaine will need a language teacher. Would you be available? I'm enclosing the Mission's address."

Matt Jr and the family were up early Monday, February 18, 1952, as the ship sighted land. In the distance Mt. Fuji stood majestic and white. In the foreground the green hills of Yokohama seemed almost to dip into the murky waters around the docks. Elaine and the children watched with excitement as dock workers came on board. They looked different from Japanese in America. She mused over their quick words to each other: *Will I ever understand them?*

A launch came and took them to the dock where they were met by a middle-aged English lady. The huge customs shed looked forbidding and cold, but her knowledge of the Japanese language whisked them through. They were soon tucked into the Mission's almost-new Dodge sedan. Matt and Elaine had not expected a British mission with Spartan tastes to have a comfortable American car.

Everything else helped them realize they were in Japan: the words everyone spoke, the leaden sky, the melting snow on the broken pavement, and the chewy little caramel candies the Mission driver bought for the children. Somehow, amid all this, the Dodge was incongruous, but the heater's warmth and the driver's friendly ways made them feel welcome.

The family was taken to a restaurant attached to the large Tokyo train station. Waitresses hovered over the two blonde, blue-eyed girls. Matt and Elaine were to discover Japanese kindness to children a never-failing joy on this island. Such tolerance, which extended beyond children to parents, would later help them draw near people, despite the language barrier.

As they drove six hours through the countryside, the family was absorbed by the sights. Fields of winter wheat struggling to grow under a blanket of melting snow. Unpainted, thatched-roof farmhouses surrounded by trees. Men hauling carts that just barely moved aside for the car. Trains in the distance rushing between Tokyo and the north-central country.

Elaine felt two emotions: a strange warmth toward the women she saw trudging along the sides of the road and a cold fear that she might not be happy here, nor fit in. Even their companion spoke a different, British, English. Only the incongruous Dodge was familiar. She pondered, *Will I, too, always be out of place?*

Late that night they reached their destination. Doors slid back to reveal a new world that was to become home. They walked into the stone-paved entry, dutifully removed their shoes and stepped into slippers waiting on the polished floor. Slippers, they soon learned, had to be taken off when stepping on the *tatami*, thick straw mats. The house was filled with new lessons. Almost at once they were taught the importance of correctly closing sliding doors. They had to move within this new world in ways that would minimize their foreignness. *I wonder if I'll ever perform properly?* thought Elaine. She could not hide her fears from Matt.

Two Japanese-style rooms in an upstairs wing of the old Mission house were set aside for the Kingsbury family. The *tokonoma*, alcove, in one of the rooms fascinated the children. "Oh, Mother, see this little cupboard," Kathy exclaimed, as she peeked behind a gilt-papered sliding door. "Can I keep my things here?"

"Mine, mine," Anne insisted, trying to reserve a dark, polished wood shelf for herself.

It had been a long day. The children snuggled down in their brightly flowered *futon*, thick cotton-padded sleeping quilts, laid out on the *tatami*. Matt and Elaine slept in a four-and-half mat room; the girls were in a six-mat one.

Next morning, after descending the stairs, they were greeted by recruits from Switzerland and Australia, then sat down to a traditional British breakfast: bland porridge, toast stacked vertically in wire "coolers," hard-boiled eggs, tea. Miss Parr opened the conversation: "Mr. Ken Nakajima, evidently an acquaintance of your father's, wrote offering to be your language teacher. He's a retired widower with a niece living 15 minutes by bicycle from Mission headquarters. We interviewed him and determined his willingness to follow the Naganuma method of teaching Japanese without the use of English, then gave him a contract. He moved from Nagaoka last week and is ready when you are."

Language lessons were the door through which Matt and Elaine went out into the world of Japanese thought. Ken became a superior guide through the delicate landscape of language. No previous study had prepared them for such pleasures. New words for everything were to be expected, but lining them up in unexpected ways challenged their Western brains. Difficulties and exceptions hid behind every rule of grammar.

Ken went to great effort to avoid the use of English. Beads of perspiration stood on his forehead while snow sifted down outside the windows. The exertion of transmitting his thoughts to adults who knew less than toddlers took its toll. He was exhausted by teatime. So were the adult toddlers trying to grow up too quickly. How could *mae* mean both "in front of" and "previously?" How could *gohan* mean a "meal" or "rice" but never "uncooked rice?" Matt and Elaine sat through long, incomprehensible sermons on Sundays, vying to see who could write down the longest list of understood words.

In the post-war years, interest in Christianity grew among young people. Even industrial Japan recognized this phenomenon. Silk mills in Gumma prefecture encouraged missionaries to introduce the Bible to hundreds of young women living in mill dormitories. After more language progress, Matt's turn to enter these mills finally came. Not wanting to go alone, he sent a post card to a friend of the Mission, a farmer living in a village an hour away. Would Mr Amada accompany Matt into the mills during slack winter months? The postcard went unanswered.

Something must be wrong. With Ken along as interpreter, Matt drove to the sleepy village. Near Amada's thatched-roof farmhouse, Matt noticed a small barn-like structure with a cross above it. As the truck pulled into the courtyard, Amada's five small children tumbled off the veranda but kept their distance from the dust-covered vehicle. Mrs Amada came out, recognized the Mission truck and said,

"My husband is out in the fields. I'll send the children for him. Make yourselves at home in the chapel. I'll bring tea and *osembei*, cookies."

Matt and Ken removed their shoes, then stepped up to the tatami floor. The barren, unheated chapel epitomized the austerity of post-war village life. They left their coats on and blew warm air into cupped hands. Soon Mrs Amada came with a charcoal brazier; its hot sides drew their stiff fingers around it. Several minutes later in walked farmer Amada, dressed in faded khaki togs and woolen cap. The children gingerly slipped in behind him. They were bundled in patched, quilted jackets and pants, the girls in red, the boys in blue. Peering from behind their parents, they stared at the strangers. Amada began:

"I didn't know how to answer your card..."

"Matt knows you are busy, but he thought you might be able to slip away one day a week during winter months," interpreted Ken.

"I'm not fit to preach to others," replied Amada. "I built this chapel to reach the villagers. Recently they stopped coming altogether. Even the Sunday school is next to nothing."

The empty chapel dramatized Amada's despair. What words from Matt could lift his spirits? He could find none. At that moment, Mrs Amada pointed to the poured green tea, the tray with *osembei* and small candies. Unexpected guests produced these morsels from her cupboards. The children's eyes turned from the visitors to the tray. With correct Japanese politeness, Matt and Ken ignored the refreshments and continued the conversation. Mrs Amada insisted, "Please take some," then picked up the tray and passed it to Ken, who took one small biscuit and passed the tray to Matt. With aplomb, Matt opened his large coat pocket, emptied the entire tray into it, and without a pause passed the empty tray to an older boy seated to his left. The children watched aghast. Younger ones began to giggle. Mrs Amada put a hand over her mouth to conceal her amusement. Amada could restrain himself no longer and broke into a wide smile. Everyone started to laugh, even Ken. The children weren't quite sure of the prank until Matt returned his pocketful of candy and *osembei* to the tray.

Outside, as Matt and Ken climbed into the truck, Amada stood with his family around him. The children were saying, "*Aba, ne*?" see you again, won't we? Then Amada surprised Matt. "Next week, stop by on your way to the mills. I'll be ready."

Didn't someone say people are more alike than cultures? mused Matt, as they drove back in silence. *Perhaps I should just be myself.*

23

Shin Nakajima had grown weary of *ronin* (leaderless) existence. A *ronin* in the Tokugawa (17th-19th centuries) era was a retainer who had lost his master; in other words, a *leaderless samurai*. The word was given heightened meaning by a 1703 incident in Edo, old Tokyo. Two years before, a Japanese baron from Ako in West Honshu drew his sword and wounded an official in the Edo castle. Such behavior drew the death penalty; the baron committed suicide by *harakiri* and his entire fiefdom was confiscated. Overnight, Ako retainers became *ronin*. Revenge, however, drove 47 of them into a desperate, long-range plan. For two years they ostensibly sank into lives of debauchery so as to keep castle authorities off guard. Then on a snowy night they stormed the residence of the official who had caused their leader's demise, killing him. Though they had public sympathy, the Tokugawa *shogun* ordered the leaderless retainers to atone for their conduct by committing *harakiri*. Whereupon the 47 Ronin, demonstrating samurai virtue to the last, lined up, disemboweled themselves, and toppled into the snow. Japanese playwrights have dramatized the episode ever since.

A modern-day *ronin* is a high school graduate seeking university admission. Until admitted, he is, well, leaderless or purposeless. For two consecutive years Shin took entrance exams at leading universities in Tokyo to no avail, despite the promptings of his father, Yuki. Shin pinned Confucian analects above his desk to motivate toward diligent preparation. He needed to. Shin was more athlete than scholar. Middle height and broad-shouldered, he excelled in *judo,* winning his black belt at the age of eighteen. Unlike his peers, however, Shin made light of that accomplishment. He laughed it off as a judge's mistake. In short, he didn't take himself or even his career seriously. There was mischief running in his veins. Whatever the discussion, in class or with friends, he always appeared on the verge of breaking out in laughter. This trait irritated friends. "Get serious, will you!" they often shouted. He refused to comb his thick curly hair and when asked his name, would send friends into laughter by pointing to the tangled mess atop his head and say, "Just call me Bird's Nest."

Would today be another disappointment? Test results were to be posted at Waseda University. Shin thought he had answered most questions, but had believed that before. In March he left the Nakajima home in Nagaoka and boarded a train for Tokyo, a four-hour journey.

Before a large bulletin board at Waseda, hundreds of candidates strained to see the names of those admitted for the year 1958. Shin's eyes ran down the list. *Not in that column. Not in the next. Wait! Could it be? Yes, clearly written, Shin Nakajima!*

He fumbled in his pocket for directions: "Take the Seibu train, get off at Higashi Fushimi, follow this map to their home. Introduce yourself to the foreign teacher. Tell him you are Yuki Nakajima's son." Shin made his way to a green house nestled among luxuriant Musashino trees. Not 30 feet away stood a two-storied, shingled structure, unpainted, functional, basic. *No doubt the student quarters,* guessed Shin. A foreign lady greeted him and read his note.

"My husband is next door with the students. I'll call him." Stepping into her shoes, Elaine walked across to the Hall stairway and called, "Matt, the grand-nephew of our language teacher is here."

"We would be happy to have you, Nakajima," said Matt after reading the note. "To have a son of the Nakajima family here is indeed a privilege. This Hall was built by a Japanese pastor, but he cannot manage it. We have just come from the country to watch over the boys."

Shin returned to Nagaoka, packed his bags and left for Waseda. A new world opened before him: new friends and new experiences, such as joining a Christian fraternity. The more he distanced himself from Nagaoka life, the more he wanted his father liberated from the past. On one return visit to Nagaoka, he dropped by to chat with Pastor Suzuki and left a request: "While I'm here, please come visit us. It's hard for me to talk to Dad." Two days later the pastor appeared in the Nakajima entryway. Yuki and Shin were there to meet him. "Please come in," they said.

"I'm delighted to meet you," began Suzuki, bowing with hands on a low table in the *tatami* room. "Shin told me about you. Your time in Manchuria. Battles you fought in China, Indonesia, and Okinawa."

"Oh, that. It's all behind me now. Have some tea and *osembei*," offered Yuki. "Shin asked me to meet you. I'm a Buddhist but don't go to the temple. Nor to

the Shrine. I've never been to church. Shin wants me to break out of my isolation, make new friends. I'm not motivated. Perhaps it was the war...."

"If I went through what you did, I'd feel the same," consoled Suzuki, trying to a get a purchase on the problem.

"Kazuko and I are surprised," continued Yuki. "Shin has changed remarkably since he got faith. But

I'm too old. How can faith change the past? I find no meaning in what I went through. That's why I avoid people and distrust government. I'm content with my job and family."

At that moment Kazuko opened the sliding paper doors, and from a kneeling position placed bowls in front of each one. Suzuki looked down at the steaming rice topped with cooked egg, onion and chicken. Taking chopsticks in hand, he began,

"Nakajima *san*, you grew up on a farm. You sowed rice and reaped harvests. Rice grains produce more rice by falling into the soil, allowing their hulls to disintegrate, to die. It's a life principle. Jesus used the grain metaphor to prepare his followers for an apparently devastating defeat, his death on a cross. He told them that through his sacrificial death God's glory would be revealed."

"Glory?"

"Yes, the word means brilliance, majesty, power. God would somehow bring light out of darkness. Er… triumph out of defeat, strength out of weakness. Jesus knew this and lived with the sign of the Cross over his heart."

"Which means?"

"He never lost sight of the life principle—his death would bring life to the world. And in accepting the humiliation of the Cross he experienced the presence of God, his glory."

"He had a choice; I didn't," protested Yuki.

"You do. I do. When life disappoints us, we can withdraw, nursing our wounds. Or, by faith we can turn defeat into victory and allow new life to spring forth, a life that is outgoing, caring, vulnerable."

24

For months after the conversation with Pastor Suzuki, Yuki pondered the strength-out-of-weakness principle. He made no headway until he called to mind examples of human weakness and how they affected him. He remembered the itinerant paper-play artist in Manchuria, weak in faith, bicycling around Changchun. *Wasn't he more courageous than the Kwangtung police?* What about the dead Chinese soldier who resembled Peng? *Didn't he make you want to quit China?* What about the defenseless lad in Indonesia who stood up for the Dutch? *Didn't he make you want to leave?* Even coming out of the cave in

Okinawa. W*eren't you strongest at the moment of defeat?*

The end of Yuki's self-imposed isolation was near. He began attending the local church, sitting alone at the back. Everything about the service was old—people in dark kimonos, tattered hymn books, Bibles covered with soiled embroidery, floors varnished the color of caramel, pulpit overlaid with light and dark-brown plywood. Behind it stood Pastor Suzuki whose hair blended into the fading black vesture, making the whole seem like one garment from head to toe.

Yet, there were sharp contrasts. From the base of the pulpit dazzling white chrysanthemum pointed upward, overarched by branches woven into a cross. A sharper contrast came when Pastor Suzuki spoke: "Faith makes us new people: cynical teachers become new teachers, old samurai become new samurai. The new samurai is released from bondage to self, in order to serve society. He is not influenced by popularity or antagonism, gain or loss. To the contrary, he is free to pour body, mind, and spirit into the task given him. His life is bound up with the lives of others. It finds its meaning there, in sharing their sufferings and joys. This is self-fulfillment, first in the Creator, then in fellow human beings. Such a life becomes a demonstration of what our ultimate goal and direction should be: fellowship, first with the Creator, then with His creatures. Sharing the Divine nature infuses us with a quality, an eternal quality, not so much in time but in depth. Our life, then, becomes preparation for that perfect life in heaven with its heightened meaning, enduring comradeship, encircling beauty, and penetrating joy."

The next week Yuki and Kazuko surprised the neighborhood by performing two sacraments. First, before the Shinto god-shelf Kazuko held a chair while Yuki climbed up with hammer and saw. From the shelf he removed pictures of ancestors, one of which was Uncle Ken sitting upright in army uniform, holding a sword in its scabbard. Small cups for food and drink were next. Out came the nails, and Yuki lowered the shelf for Kazuko to hold. They went quietly out in their small garden. Yuki poured kerosene over the shelf and good luck charms, then lit a flame.

Secondly, they went with Pastor Suzuki to the banks of the Chikuma River. Believers held up a cotton sheet for the couple to change into white baptismal garments. Yuki emerged first and walked slowly into the swirling stream. Pastor Suzuki held Yuki's nose and mouth with a white kerchief and then plunged him backward into the water, saying "I baptize you, Yuki, in the name of the Father, the

Son, and the Holy Spirit." Believers were singing as Yuki walked out dripping and Kazuko waded in: "In the cross, in the cross, Be my glory ever, Till my raptured soul shall find rest beyond the river."

25

Yuki's tranquil Nagaoka life was interrupted a few months later by a company request. *Mitsubishi* was expanding its markets in China; would Yuki go to Shanghai and negotiate an export license? Yuki was pleased at the suggestion; he assumed his bilingual capability prompted their request. On such a trip he might visit Yinhan Peng, his boyhood chum from Changchun days. Peng was now teaching Japanese at the Shanghai Construction Academy. *I can ask Yin to translate promotional material for Japanese imports.*

Peng had returned to Tokyo from Manchuria in 1935, entered university in the early 1940s, then was conscripted for military duty in 1945. The war ended before he saw combat. Thereafter, Peng did odd jobs in Tokyo but in 1951 returned to Keio University for graduate work. He completed his MA in economics the same year Chinese premier Zhou Enlai appealed to Chinese entrepreneurs and scholars living abroad, asking that they come help rebuild the "new China." Peng was one of twelve-hundred overseas Chinese who responded, sailing for China in the Fall of 1953. He rose steadily in the academic ranks and married a Shanghai girl. Unable to cope with his sudden bursts of anger, she moved out of his apartment after their first child was born.

The political climate and economic situation in China were less than ideal when Yuki's trip was scheduled. The Great Leap Forward of 1958 had wreaked havoc on China's rural economy, bringing misery to millions. Central planning broke down, the transportation system was disrupted, yields spiraled downward and peasants were worked to the point of exhaustion. Three years of bad weather made matters worse. By 1959 critical food shortages had reduced the flow of meat and produce to the cities. All of China was in the grips of a major depression.

The free world watched. Could Chinese communism feed its people? Few Japanese firms would risk involvement. *Mitsubishi Foods* was the exception: their representative, Yuki Nakajima, boarded a Shanghai-bound ship from Niigata. Cadres from Shanghai's Central Planning Committee stood to their feet as Yuki walked into the reception lounge. The familiar tea table with carved wooden dragon legs and the soiled linen covers hiding rumpled deep cushion chairs made

Yuki feel at home. His hosts, however, appeared taken aback to see Yinhan Peng at his side. Eyebrows were raised higher when Yuki announced he didn't need their assigned lodging but would stay in Peng's apartment.

"My interpreter, Yinhan Peng—an old friend from Changchun," began Yuki. There was complete silence.

"We have our own interpreter, Mr Shi, seated on your left. Thank you all the same, Mr Peng."

Characteristically, Peng could not conceal his anger: "Well, if I'm not needed, let me be excused. I've work to do back at the Academy."

That evening, after supper in the Academy's faculty dining room, Peng took Yuki on a tour of the campus. At a corner outside the central quadrangle, they dropped into the campus co-op. Emerging from the store, their eyes were blinded by a camera flash. Someone with a marked limp tucked a camera into his faded blue Mao-jacket, mounted a bicycle, and pedaled out the main gate.

"Was he taking our picture?" asked Yuki.

"I have no idea," replied Peng, visibly shaken. "Perhaps you'd better move to the assigned lodging."

This episode threw a pall over Yuki's trip. He turned over the promotional material to Mr Shi, asked Central Planning to review and sign a prepared contract, and then caught the next ship back to Niigata. His coming to China may have enhanced Mitsubishi's future, but did it embarrass Peng?

26

Peng was preparing fish tempura and omelette for his little girl. Everything was ready by 6:30 p.m., but the matron had not brought her. A sixth sense told Peng something had gone wrong. Feeling depressed, he sat at his desk, translating modern Chinese poetry into Japanese for Matsunaga Goichi's work, *Minzoku Shijin*, Folk Poets. The room was dark by now, for it was past seven. Still neither matron nor daughter appeared. *Perhaps I should call*, Peng thought, until he remembered that public phones did not operate after 6:00 p.m. Growing impatient, he paced around the hardwood floor of the 12- by 18-foot room. The large wall to the south was mostly window. Every time he passed it he would glance down at the gate entrance, lit by a street lamp, but could see no one.

Why do the white walls seem so somber today? Why doesn't the matron bring her? Peng mused while the fried fish and omelette got cold. *Oh, well, I'm not hungry anyway. Perhaps I should look for her at the school.* Peng glanced at his watch: 7:30 p.m. *I'll wait until 8:00 p.m., then go.* Reclining on the sofa, Peng turned on the radio. All that could be heard was martial music, so he switched it off.

Suddenly there was a knock. Thinking he would take her in his arms, Peng pulled open the door. There stood two policemen in white uniform. Standing directly behind them were two detectives dressed in dark tan suits. All four men entered his room. Without uttering a word, one plainclothes-man, about 25 years old, placed a white sheet of paper on Peng's desk. In large characters was written, *House search warrant by the People's District Court of Shanghai,* followed by an official seal. Peng scrutinized the paper, thinking it must be a case of mistaken identity. There was no mistake. Peng's name was clearly written there. "Go ahead. Search anywhere you wish," he told them.

The search began with Peng's desk, which had four drawers on either side and one in the middle. One detective turned to the left drawers, pulled the top one out, and pushed it back. Next he pulled open the second in which were several hundred unused index cards. He flipped through them rapidly until he found one and pulled it out. Five Arabic numerals were written on it.

"What's this?" he asked.

"I don't know," answered Peng. "The cards were bought just last month. I haven't used them yet. It's strange those numbers are written there."

"What's so strange about that? Don't pretend to be ignorant," he shot back. "It's the secret telephone number of Shanghai's Military Command Board." With that the desk search ended. Eight hundred pages of modern Chinese poetry translated into Japanese lay in the right desk drawer, but he gave them not a glance.

The entire investigation lasted two and a half hours, most of it spent examining Peng's book collection. Moving according to plan, one detective produced a prepared summons notice from his briefcase. "You will have to come to the Public Security Bureau office. Make preparations immediately."

"How long will it take? It's already quite late."

"You should be through in two or three hours."

"Then I need not take overnight things?"

"No. You'll need nothing. Come as you are."

Peng changed into the suit he had made for graduation from Tokyo's Keio University, put his wallet in the inside pocket, then left the room with them. A jeep was waiting outside. Peng glanced around but saw no one else as the two detectives boarded the jeep with him. A gentle breeze cooled

Peng's perspiring forehead as they drove along. He was upset but somehow believed after a few hours he would be homeward bound, borne along by the same breeze. In five or six minutes, the jeep brought them to the district office of Shanghai's Public Security Bureau. They drove through the gate.

Dismounting the jeep, Peng was taken to the waiting room of the district office, kept waiting for 30 minutes and then hauled off to a steel-barred room of the detention ward. At a desk inside sat a uniformed guard with a pistol strapped to his waist. He rose to his feet, opened the steel door and then led Peng to an inner room having table and chairs.

Shortly thereafter a man dressed in a faded blue Mao-jacket came in, carrying a large packet but walking with a noticeable limp. Peng immediately recalled the camera-flash incident on campus. With an ominous look the man stood at attention, staring at Peng.

"Are you Yinhan Peng ?"

"Yes."

"The error you have committed is graver than that of the rightists. We have everything right here," he said, pointing to a folder twelve inches square and one inch thick on which were written in bold characters, "Personal Profile Dossier."

A dossier is kept on every director, staff member, and worker. In it appears data such as place of birth, career, thought condition, etc. Anyone with some position in Chinese society is shadowed by this dossier all his life. His political post or possibility for advancement is determined by its contents. Lower level staff members and workers call it a *jin gang quan*. The *jin gang quan* was a headband on the monkey *Sun Wukong* who appears in the fable *Xiyou*. Whenever *Sun Wukong* would not obey the priest *Tang Seng*, the latter would chant a sutra, causing the band to tighten excruciatingly around the monkey's head. For years the Communist Party has used this dossier to exact total compliance from the Chinese people. Peng was alarmed by the remarks of the man holding his dossier but, regaining composure, queried him, "The error graver than that of the rightists to which you refer, what is it?"

"That's yours to confess." Pointing to the dossier, he added, "It's all in here."

Peng was stupefied. After a pause the interrogator grinned, saying, "I won't say you betrayed your country. But you're not a patriot. You just put on a patriotic front. You have a number of views about us in the Personnel Section, don't you?"

"What has that to do with rightist errors? Is that a crime graver than that of the rightists?" Peng asked. The interrogator kept silent, so Peng pressed the

conversation a step further: "Let me ask a question. I was called here by a summons notice. After telling me that it would be over after two or three hours of questioning, they put me in this detention ward. Isn't that illegal?"

"Illegal? What do you mean? It is you who are to confess the error of your ways. We shall get to the matter after you confess and carry out self criticism. You know full well the policy of the Party." Saying this, he left the room. Not knowing what to do, Peng sat there blankly, waiting for the time to pass. Finally a guard came in with hands out and demanded, "Let's have your valuables. Also, the belt from your trousers." As soon as Peng turned these over to him, he was led to one of the steel barred cells. The guard unlocked a rusty door and said, "All right, in you go," pointing inside.

The crowded ward was 9 by 15 feet wide, covered with wood paneling. The ward leader somehow made enough room for Peng to creep in and lie down between fifteen inmates. He laid down but couldn't sleep, not because of restless tossing but inability to move. Before long a reveille bell sounded. Each inmate rose and began folding his blanket. Next, they all lined up for the morning toilet routine. On the floor near the steel door was a huge, wooden bucket. When one of them yelled, *Finished*! a guard would hand him a thick sheet of rough, yellowish brown paper, woven out of straw. Peng thought it strange that so few were having bowel movements, but learned later it was because they were ingesting so little food. Bathroom chores over, they all sat cross legged on the floor, single file around the four walls of the ward. Sixteen men sitting shoulder to shoulder around the room completely filled it. Peng was kept there three months; it was always full.

Breakfast, a huge barrel of rice gruel, was finally brought in and set down by the steel door. The rice gruel was ladled into army-type open canteens, filling them almost to the brim. As a side dish, seven or eight radish slices the size of toothpicks were piled on top. Peng stared at his canteen, wondering how he could consume that much. Just then he was startled out of his brown study by the sound of pouring rain and looked up only to discover all the inmates slurping gruel in unison. What a shock to one who had been taught from childhood never to speak during meals, never to emit a sound while eating. Before long, however, Peng became accustomed to the spectacle. The strangeness of making a racket while slurping gruel wore off; in fact, he came to think it the most enjoyable way to devour gruel.

Peng didn't feel like eating that first meal, so turned it over to the ward leader. He divided it among the others, two of whom quickly acknowledged the favor with a cordial look. Out of earshot of the guard, they opened up a conversation:

"You a returnee?" Peng nodded affirmatively but said nothing.

"When did you get back?"

"1953."

"You must be one of those patriotic returnees. Why on earth, then...?" He bit his tongue. Apparently no one was supposed to get that personal. The two exchanged glances and smiled. From that moment on all the inmates gave Peng friendly looks. The next day their conversation continued. They seemed hungry for knowledge of other countries.

"From which country did you return?"

"Japan."

"You can write Japanese sentences using Chinese characters, then?" Peng nodded but said nothing.

"Can you express what you're thinking now in Japanese?"

"Of course."

Intrigued, one inmate pressed Peng further. "I've seen Chinese characters in Japanese sentences but have never seen someone write Japanese. Would you mind writing a sentence for me?"

"I have no paper or pen."

The inmate quickly produced both. Peng took his pen and wrote several lines from a Japanese poem that expressed the freedom of birds, using only Japanese phonetic script. The entire ward was fascinated to see writing in which there were no Chinese characters. They took turns looking at the poem.

A guard summoned Peng out of the ward several days later and thrust the poem in front of him.

"What's this?"

"A poem about the freedom of birds."

"What's the point of writing things like that? Forget it! Yours is to make a confession. Without delay."

"Oh, I see. Sorry. From now on I'll be more careful."

Luckily, he was one of the nicer guards. Peng forced a smile, then returned to the ward. A look around reminded him that early that morning one inmate had left the ward. *No doubt my informer.*

The same afternoon they summoned the ward leader who, upon return, issued a statement on regulations:

"From now on, exercise care in the following: One, don't discuss among yourselves circumstances surrounding your crime or details of your error. Two, don't show what you write on paper to anyone else. Three, do not exchange names or addresses. Violators will be punished."

The inmates cherished one diversion from the humdrum of ward life: basking in the sun once a week. "Basking in the sun" was their euphemism for the mandatory weekly exercise period. Actually they did no exercise. They merely lined up outside in a small yard for a brief period and gulped down great drafts of fresh air. Without it, the government would have had sick inmates on their hands.

Their delight, however, was the guards' headache, for on a previous outing several inmates had escaped. Now, a surly guard with malevolent eyes kept them under strict surveillance. Since only two of the five wards could bask at one time, three rotations lasting 30 minutes each were required. But that consumed 90 minutes of the guard's time. Finding that unacceptable, he reduced their basking time to 10 minutes and insisted they hurry out and back. Inmates who dawdled lost their basking right that day; those who talked found theirs cancelled the following week. In such capricious ways lower echelon officials administering tiniest grants of freedom from above shrank them tinier still by making prisoners feel obligated or by attaching self serving conditions to every privilege.

This "freedom shrinking" pervades not only detention wards but government institutions, schools, and industry. "If the top beam be warped, the lower one becomes twisted" has become a household phrase since the Cultural Revolution. In a country like China, which for centuries has stressed unquestioning submission to authority, those in the lower echelon find it difficult to make independent judgments on good and evil, justice and injustice. They have found that blind imitation of those above is the safest course to follow.

27

Days were getting cooler. Time to move. Peng was summoned out of his cell, given a hasty haircut that made him look like a Buddhist monk, and issued a duffle bag containing blanket and toiletries. A total of eight inmates with shaven heads were loaded into an escort vehicle. As they peered through the steel barred window of the moving van, the streets of Shanghai looked especially poignant. The van went east along Huaibai Street and turned north over Waibaidu Bridge. After that, with all eight vying to catch a glimpse of the route, Peng could not make out where they were going.

The best part of the trip was being able to talk openly with one another, though only two or three felt free to do so. The others may have grown accustomed to the rule against fraternizing or were reluctant to speak to strangers. Upon arrival, they were disgorged on to a spacious yard in front of some barracks. A policeman led them inside where they put down their luggage; he gave the order: "Select any spot you wish and rest a while."

While other prisoners milled around, Peng stood by the faucet near the entryway, brushing teeth, washing hands and face with soap for the first time in months. A twenty year-old youth named Chen was standing nearby. Lending him soap and towel, Peng remarked,

"What's freedom? Freedom is space! Freedom is being able to talk!"

With a puzzled look, Chen replied, "Do you think so?"

Twenty minutes later, Peng returned to the barracks only to discover young Chen reclining against his duffle bag. "Don't you want to have a look around outside?" Peng asked.

"I was keeping track of your luggage," Chen said, then rushed outside. Within minutes he returned, calling out, "Everyone's lined up in front of the office telephone. Aren't you going to put through a call?"

Peng thought he might request Shanghai friends to bring him an enamel rice bowl but gave up the idea when he learned they registered all visitors. "What about you?" he asked.

"I have no family back home. I couldn't expect friends to come this far."

"What'll you do for blankets?"

"As soon as we know our destination, I'll write asking friends to send them."

Chen related to Peng that his father had passed away several years ago. His mother, a Christian, had been deported to a labor camp in Anhui. Chen was the only child. "What frauds!" he had remarked to several acquaintances. "The Communists guarantee religious freedom in the constitution while going about closing churches, arresting pastors and believers." Someone informed authorities. He ended up in the same Shanghai detention ward as Peng but in a different cell. Now they were together.

Just then they heard shouts, "Here they come! "Here they come!" Pandemonium broke loose. Into the barracks came several cooks bearing steamed rice in a huge barrel two feet in diameter. When the commotion died down, one cook read out names one by one. Each went in turn to receive a ball of rice slightly larger than a man's fist. The snack contained a teaspoonful of pickles. Peng put his on a handkerchief so as not to lose a grain while munching away. It was another "first" in three months. The more he nibbled, the sweeter it tasted. The rice ball wasn't all that small but vanished in his stomach without a trace. Someone called out, "Taking water afterwards makes you feel full." Sure enough, water brought the same full sensation that had come after slurping rice gruel in the detention ward.

Talk shifted to conditions in Jiangxi and Anhui. Friendly conversation animated the barracks. They were like kids going on a school excursion. From the absence of gloomy expressions no one could have guessed they were prisoners. The majority had been unemployed idlers. Being rounded up and taken to the staging center relieved them of worry about their next meal. The place of exile was of no consequence. Peng engaged Chen in conversation,

"How did you come to believe in Christianity?"

"My mother believes. I followed her steps."

"What's the attraction of Christian faith?"

"The teachings of Christ help us through suffering."

"How do you answer the communists who say religion is an opiate that deadens the revolutionary spirit?"

"That's the Party's insult to all religion," added Chen. "Those deniers of religion forget they have a religion of their own—faith in communism. They say communism will bring about heaven on earth but can't tell us what it will look like."

"You've got a point. We can't take much comfort from the present. The first stage of communism, our so-called socialist society, has been a bitter experience for the majority."

"No matter how much they ban religion, religious faith will never die."

"I look at it this way," Peng said. "Eyeing the future, one must endure in the present. I find it difficult to be patient but intend to try."

"My mother," added Chen, "taught me these words from the Bible: 'The light shines on in darkness and the darkness is not able to extinguish it.'"

"Exactly. We must persevere, confident that in 10 or 20 years the light will overcome the darkness. Difficult days lie ahead. But no matter how grim our situation, we must learn to cope. The canny fighter stays alive. Just to survive will be a victory for us."

"Won't it be good if they send you and me to the same camp? I have a feeling they will," said Chen.

"Fine with me. One sympathetic person along is reassuring. But keep our discussion to yourself."

On the evening of the fourth day plain clothesmen swarmed into the barracks and had everyone stand in formation. With a name list in hand one barked out commands. "We'll now form you into a company. Yours, the 4th Company, will be made up of four platoons having four squads each."

Saying this, he read off the names in each squad and the appointed squad leader. Platoon leaders and company commanders were police whose names were not read. Was it the better part of wisdom to keep them anonymous? Peng and Chen were put into the last squad of the fourth platoon, apparently bound for the same place. The man continued,

"Tomorrow morning you will be going to Jiangxi. Rise at six, ready to depart at seven. You'll be given two rice balls each. When to eat them is up to you. Those who ignore law and order en route will be severely punished. Understand?"

When they left, Chen danced a jig. He assured Peng that Jiangxi was superior to Qinghai, Gansu, or Anhui. Geographically, it is the closest to Shanghai. Six hours by express, one passes through Zhejiang province and then arrives at Jiangxi. Distances to East Jiangxi and West Jiangxi, however, vary considerably. Pondering their destination, Peng crawled under his blanket. His thoughts flew to Shanghai and his missing daughter. *Where is she? Why no word?* Chen called out, "Jiangxi isn't all that far. Your friends can come see you."

"But, if my friends come, they'll invite suspicion." Just then Peng realized he would lose all touch with Yuki Nakajima and Goichi Matsunaga, the Japanese poet. The prospects of being cut off from such friends made it one of his bleaker moments. Wondering how many years would elapse before seeing them again, Peng dropped off to sleep.

28

Departure was suddenly moved ahead 30 minutes. To reach their destination before sundown, they must depart without a moment's delay. In the midst of last-minute preparations a plainclothesman entered the barracks and called out, "Now hear this! You'll be going by truck to the Shanghai Station. Squad leaders, keep your men firmly in hand. The truck moves at high speed. Take care. A few days ago one prisoner leaped out to make a getaway. He died on the way to hospital. If you want to end your life that way, that's your business. Understand?"

This gave hint that a getaway from the moving truck was possible. But hopes were dashed when boarding began; as precaution against escape the inmates were packed in till they couldn't move. Quickly gathering momentum, the truck sped along deserted Shanghai streets. Few cars were on the road, since it was before the morning rush hour. Within 10 minutes they arrived at the station. Though Communist forces had entered Shanghai 11 years previously, the depot had undergone little change. The noticeable difference was the absence of neon signs and prostitutes roaming around.

They were herded along a platform lined with police and soldiers holding rifles aslant. Nearly 1,000 inmates had been formed into sixteen platoons, totaling 64 squads. These were now funneled into cattle cars of a waiting freight. Being the last formed, Peng and Chen's squad had but twelve men. They scrambled into one boxcar that reeked of cattle and horses. Straw was strewn all over. No windows meant no clues as to the train's route.

Within moments the train gave a jolt. They were off! Having been awakened early that morning, the men bedded down quickly. Blankets cushioned them on the wooden car bed and made the trip tolerable. Peng laid down but couldn't drop off because of the click clack of the rails. At 1:00 p.m. the train pulled into Shangrao City, lying in the eastern part of Jiangxi province. It had covered 300 miles at 48 miles per hour, faster than any civilian express. After a 20 minute stop, it started up again, covering the next 240 miles in five hours. They arrived at Xinyu after 6:00 p.m. Peng was relieved when ordered to detrain. At least they hadn't been exiled to some mountainous backwater. Xinyu lies 28 degrees north of the equator on the 115th longitude, 560 miles southwest of Shanghai. As such it has a warmer climate than Shanghai, another cause for thanks.

Shouldering his duffle bag, Peng alighted from the boxcar. Standing in formation along the roofless platform were more than 50 infantrymen with fixed bayonets. One look at their facial features and clothes told Peng they had not accompanied them from Shanghai. This was confirmed when they barked out commands:

"Quit stalling!" "Get a move on!" Their unmistakable Jiangxi accent raised fears they would be even more uncouth than their Shanghai counterparts. After roll-call the inmates set off under these escorts, advancing in columns of four. Flashlight-bearing riflemen, positioned 10 yards apart on each side of Peng's company, marched alongside. As the platoon drew away from the station, Peng could tell that the armed escorts numbered closer to a 100, not 50.

They trudged along at dusk. Peng's duffle bag was getting heavier by the minute. Evening stillness was broken by frequent shouts from the van and rear: "Keep moving!" Shanghai legs were no match for Jiangxi ones. "Commander, we can't keep this up much longer!" cried out some, but their pleas fell to the ground. In the twilight they approached a dark steel mill. *This is it*, Peng thought, but after a five-minute break they set off once more. Just then Chen suggested Peng and he switch packs. That was a timely offer. Peng's duffle bag was unmanageably large; the road had become full of potholes.

Shortly after 8:00 p.m. a small hill came into view; they staggered up the steep embankment. Their difficulty was not distance but covering it with legs unaccustomed to bearing loads and already weakened by confinement. Before them to the right stood two white walled, low dwellings. They were lit by an unusually bright lamp dangling from a power line pole. Directly in front, another such light illuminated an expansive yard. Across it they could make out three huge sheds with black roofs and no walls. After another roll-call, each company was ordered to enter a shed and then bed down in platoon formation. Someone spoke up:

"Commander, where are the tap and toilets?"

"Running water? Where do you think you are? Toilets? Use the corner of the yard," he snapped.

Tension mounted. "Commander, how about some rice soup? We've had nothing to drink since morning."

"You've been given today's ration. Where'll the rice come from?"

"Who cares if some of tomorrow's rice goes for tonight's soup? Why not practice humanitarian ideals of the revolution on us? We're human too. How did the commanders fare for lunch? We saw steam rising from your rice pots. Surely you won't begrudge us a cup of soup? What are we here for? Re-education or physical abuse? Tell us!" No one broke ranks. The company stood as one man confronting the commander.

"Quiet down, all of you. So you've had nothing to drink all day. I'll have the cook prepare rice soup. It'll take over an hour. Meanwhile, lay out your bed rolls and rest. I'll let you know when the soup's ready," he yelled.

The commotion died down. There was nothing in the shed except a wide dirt floor. They all stood staring, not knowing what to make of it. There must be boards or straw somewhere. *Do they expect us to sleep on the bare ground? That's going too far. In their eyes we're not human beings*, thought Chen, then let out a shout, "Tyrants! They treat us worse than animals. How can we sleep here?"

"You're wasting time asking how," retorted another. "There's nothing we can do but save our protest for tomorrow and sleep on the ground tonight. Prepare to bed down. Remember, things could be worse. We're not in an open field. We have a roof over our heads."

Groaning and sighs continued for a time but finally subsided. Everyone was exhausted. It was no good just standing there, so Chen and Peng spread their blankets over duffle bags and bedded down. Chen remarked, "You said re-education through hard labor was an administrative measure. Perhaps we'd have been better off sentenced, then packed off to prison."

"How could we have foreseen this?" said Peng. "We don't know what a day may bring forth. That's life. You laugh one moment, cry the next. But if we don't find a little good in the bad, we won't last long. No matter how tough the road, we keep going." Peng felt he was talking more to himself than to Chen.

29

Peng's company bivouacked on a bank of the Yuanshui, a hundred yard-wide river flowing northeast. The Yuanshui flows from south to north, passing Nanchang City, then spilling into gigantic Poyang Lake. The day after arrival on September 18th, Peng peered down from the hilltop to the shallow river. Its bed seemed to undulate on the water surface. Nearby natural springs fed the river; rock and sand kept it as clear as well water. The southern cliff rose sheer from the river; to get down to the water, one had to make his way along a steep slope. The only egress from the hilltop area itself appeared to be along the sloping path Peng had climbed the previous night. The river served as southern boundary to the camp. Those selected for K. P. duty were to fetch water from the river with buckets slung from a *biandan*, the traditional Chinese shoulder pole. They would descend and ascend along that slope many times daily, bearing 110 pound water loads.

Taking rice bowl in hand, Peng lined up with the others before the thatched bamboo dining hall. The evening sun shone on the Yuanshui River. In the distance, smoke was rising gently from kitchen fires of peasant homes. But here they were, standing in line, forlorn beggars. Feelings of desolation welled up. *Why so melancholy? Keep a stiff upper lip! You'll make it.* Places rarely depressed Peng. Yet mixed feelings of sadness and vexation were getting the better of him. *Why didn't you investigate the true China before coming? What made you do such a rash thing?* Then his rational self echoed back less harshly: *no search from the outside could have uncovered the facts.*

"Hey, returnee! Sand hauling from tomorrow. How about some extra gruel?" The cook's voice brought Peng to himself. Anyone could tell he was a returnee by the one business suit he kept wearing. *How can I work in this suit? I must have a Mao jacket sent right away.* After supper he bought paper and envelope from the camp store and then got off a letter.

Next morning, as soon as the whistle blew, Commander Wang had all platoons fall into formation. "Attention! Dress right! Sound out your number!" he barked, then took roll call. An ex-military man from Fujian province, Wang wore cap and uniform without insignia. "Forward march!" he yelled.

Shouldering *biandan* like rifles, Peng's platoon descended the slope, then scrambled in all directions over the dry part of the riverbed. The men exchanged smiles in high spirits. At least they could move about in open space. Each squad gathered around its one man with a shovel. He would select drier areas and then commence filling baskets with sand.

"That should do it," he'd say. With baskets full they would amble one hundred yards from channel bed to hillside and dump sand in a central area, leaving enough room for trucks from the industrial complex to maneuver. More experienced ones would dart effortlessly underneath bouncing *biandan* laden with sand-filled baskets, empty their load, then return to the riverbed at a walk. Peng couldn't synchronize bounce with gait, so plodded through the sand with drooping *biandan*. Carrying sand at a walk adds to the misery, but Peng had no strength to run. Within 30 minutes his shoulders ached. Four months of confinement had all but drained his physical strength. When the pain got extreme, he would shift the pole to his left shoulder, which in turn ached severely after two or three trips. The first hour left Peng not a little anxious. *You've got no choice. Keep plodding!* After two hours the whistle signaled a break. Peng called out to Chen, "There must be an easier way."

"We've hardly begun," Chen replied. "The sand won't get lighter. Remember the saying, 'The longer the road, the heavier the load.' Ignore the shoulder ache. Practice by bouncing your pole while you run in place. In a few weeks the pain will ease."

"Really?" said Peng. "Guess we can put up with anything for two weeks. I could tolerate the whole re-education program if the end were in sight. Local peasants must run along with loads double ours."

"Triple is more like it," countered Chen.

Peng got through the first morning, somehow bolstering his spirit while nursing shoulder aches. By late afternoon pain in both shoulders became acute, not to mention a parched throat. He then recalled how a karate teacher taught him to slake thirst by placing his tongue against upper gums, causing saliva to run down the throat. This brought some relief, but shoulder aches intensified as the day wore on. *Think of it as getting your shoulders in shape*, he consoled himself.

By the next day, severe muscular ache spread from shoulder to legs. Peng tried to get the *biandan* rhythm by bouncing the pole while running in place; by late afternoon he got the knack of it. His skin seemed to be cracking, but he could feel nothing by touch. Work over, Peng wound his way back to the hilltop, dragging stiff legs along. He just managed to make it over the rise.

The first week passed. Peng had toughened his right shoulder. His pole bounced in rhythm with his step. Shoulder aches continued but surprisingly lessened when he ran. As leg pain decreased, he gained confidence. By the second week he was carrying loads with the right shoulder only. In the evenings he would feel both shoulders; muscles on the right were more pronounced. He then began building up his left shoulder. By the third week he scarcely noticed which side he was using. Leg discomfort diminished further. To his surprise Peng experienced joy that flows from misery endured.

30

The camp was struck by an epidemic of explosive dysentery, immobilizing three hundred men. Rumors spread that they had eaten spoiled meat on New Year's day; the thumb-sized daily meat ration had been doubled for that occasion. Peng's stomach became painfully distended, and five to ten times daily he passed mucuous with bloody stools. Penicillin had little effect. To make matters worse, dysentery was so endemic in Jiangxi province that their hosts thought nothing of it. Only a temperature of 102′ exempted one from work. Peng kept hauling sand while his condition deteriorated. By the month's end he was nothing but skin and bone. Extreme malnutrition, loss of body fat, dehydration, and environmental conditions unfit for cattle turned the whole company into phantoms of their former selves. The spectacle of haggard, emaciated bodies covered with grime, staggering over the dry riverbed, simply would not go into words.

As the days wore on, parched skin on inmate limbs turned dark and leathery. From hand to elbow, cracks and fissures opened, making the back of their hands look like black tortoise shells. No amount of scrubbing helped. When their hands were wet, the fissures would disappear; when dry, reappear. Some in Peng's platoon held out clenched fists together in a row. The illusion of tortoise shells lined up brought a few wry smiles. Peng stared in terror. His own hand loomed as a tortoise shell for divining the future, a practice used in ancient China. *Do those cracks portend imminent doom?*

Explosive dysentery left them dehydrated and the whole camp unsanitary. Three hundred men were defecating bloody stools in open latrines. As victims increased, the frequency of penicillin shots decreased. Seeing bloody excrement in the latrines, peasants refused to carry off night soil. Latrines overflowed. No one dared approach to clean them. Prisoners not yet stricken would avoid their use. So, during 10-minute breaks from sand hauling, they would move away from work areas and defecate in the channel. Those sick, unable to use the overflowing latrines, followed suit. The channel bed, littered with bloody feces, turned into pink sand. How nauseating! For years to come that wretched scene would flash across Peng's mind.

It staggers belief that such conditions could prevail in the twentieth century. The camp doctor reported four hundred victims, nearly 40 percent of the battalion. Though water and spoiled meat were suspected, the actual cause remained a mystery.

Peng tried to fight off its debilitating effects, but after a month his health completely broke down. Only with great effort could he, cane in hand, totter from the barrack to fetch his daily rice gruel. While swatting lice in his infested bed, Peng assessed their alarming situation. The end seemed near. Whenever he stumbled over to the latrines, the whole camp appeared hellish beyond imagination. *Perhaps*, Peng thought, *it's their way of getting rid of us. But we've not yet been convicted. Before death should come sentencing. It makes no sense.* The camp doctor's explanation seemed more plausible: he could prescribe penicillin only in half dosages because of acute shortages. If everyone were given correct amounts, the epidemic would pass. Peng had overheard someone say, "We're up against it. Medical supplies from Shanghai have been drastically cut. Until deaths are reported, those responsible won't take our situation seriously."

At last three prisoners died, one of whom, a former member of the Guomindang, slept not 10 yards from Peng. The day they carried him out on a stretcher Peng sent off a letter to a Shanghai friend, requesting special medicine for dysentery.

By February the entire labor battalion had fallen on hard times. Malnourished, overworked, crippled by dysentery, half of the thousand man battalion had wasted to nothing. Mid February found over one hundred men bedridden, unable to move. Eight men perished. Each week someone was borne out on a stretcher. Peng presumed bodies were carted to a local crematory; they could hardly be thrown into the river. It was anyone's guess why their disposal was kept secret.

Fortunately, in late February an ample supply of anti-dysentery medicine came; Peng's dysentery was arrested. Feeling better, he strolled with cane to the brow of the hill, inhaling the fresh air. There he was shocked to see several men dragging themselves along on legs swollen elephant size. Whether this was related to malfunctioning kidneys or not, he didn't know. Standing there alone Peng gazed into the far distance, entranced by the majestic landscape. In the southwesterly direction lay Mt. Jinding and Mt. Gaotianya of the Wukong Range, whose easternmost foothills rise above the plain 18 miles from the camp. He could make out famous Mt. Jinggang over 100 miles down the same range. When he turned north, enormous green swells seemed to roll toward him, whole mountain ranges tumbling one upon another from higher altitudes. Sixty miles in the same direction Mt. Wumei jutted up from the Jiuling Range like an island out of the sea. Closer by, crystal-clear streams laced through the blue green hills. This vast wilderness lay as undeveloped in 1961 as it had been since the dawn of history. Ah, Peng thought, if some conscientious regime could get China on its economic feet, a beautiful environment stands waiting for the people. What irony! The road promising such Edens seems headed for the desert.

Springtime comes early in the southern reaches of the Yangtze. Beginning in February huge cloud-columns pick up speed, then race overhead, their silent rush punctuated by thunderclaps and lightning. Overcast weather returns for a spell until suddenly a washed out sky unveils distant blue ranges. Yesterday's leaden cover bursts in frenzied movement today—towering cloud masses on the march, announcing the advent of spring or summer. Peng wondered if the insensitive rogues manipulating inmates were not hidden behind those clouds, continually changing the weather from fair to foul to keep them on edge!

On this unforgettable day, as late afternoon showers poured down, out from boiling black clouds shot hundreds of lightning bolts through the sky, great white shafts that bridged heaven and earth. Before Peng, a rainbow rose from the Yuanshui River, and then arched out to the Wukong Range. Like black peonies, numberless small clouds wafted along, variegated in color from white to grey to black. Out of every flower core emerged filaments, bundles of light, each a different shade. Peng stood on the brow of the hill, lost in admiration at the brilliant sky dappled by three dimensional peony-like clouds. Words could not portray that flamboyant scene, those dancing black clouds pierced by shafts of light. The riot of color racing by epitomized life's evanescence. *Yes,* thought Peng, *as the Chinese proverb has it, "No matter how fierce the fire blazes in the field, its smoke vanishes as a puff in the sky" Yet the beauty of the moment emblazoned on our memory triumphs over the ephemeral.*

31

To the south of the Yangtze lies the huge Poyang Lake. Major rivers of Jiangxi province—the Ganjian, the Xiushui, the Pojiang, the Xinjiang—flow into the Poyang, then along a wide delta into the Yangtze. The Poyang itself covers an area of 900 square miles. During monsoon season the area nearly doubles in size. Labor-reform barracks were built on a dry-bed area of the lake, the very area likely to be inundated during a flood. The lake itself is about 60 feet in elevation and 50 feet at its deepest point. When one climbs to Lushan from Jiujiang city, Poyang Lake is seen in the far distance, shrouded by mist. The area extending north of the lakeshore all the way to the southwest corner of Anhui Province is called the Poyang Basin. En route to Poyang the rivers deposit great amounts of silt and sand in the basin, turning it into an alluvial plain of over 7,000 square miles. The greater part of this basin is no more than 150 feet in elevation. Underground rivers keep the soil well watered. The fertile basin is known for its rice and marine products.

The day after arrival Peng's battalion learned they would be working in the Henhu Farm area. Henhu Farm is located 25 miles north by northwest of Nanchang city. Its vast farming area borders the western side of the Poyang and the eastern bank of the Ganjian River. To the south were the huge Zhugang and Chengxin farms which, together with Henhu, provided agricultural tasks for carrying out labor re-education and labor reform. Around the entire lake were more than 50 such farms. Twenty to thirty-thousand men had been sentenced to hard labor in them. Also, over 50,000 soldiers expelled from the People's Liberation Army were serving sentences of hard labor in the vicinity. Military men who retained their military rank were also being "reclaimed" on the farms.

From their barracks, 1,000 inmates marched to a small segment of the canal bank built in the past by tens of thousands of men. Using *biandan* and woven baskets, Peng's battalion was to raise and widen a segment of an irrigation canal that had crumbled after rain and flooding. From a level spot 50 yards away they began hoisting soil in baskets up the earthen dam. Within an hour, half the men started to wobble as they ascended the bank. There was no way a company of middle aged men could keep pace with the others; their efficiency fell off rapidly. Word soon got to Commander Wang. He quickly selected 40 men of strong physique from another company to serve as pacers. With large baskets of mud slung between bamboo *biandan*, they nimbly ascended and descended the bank. Wang shouted out to the others, "See how they do it? Let's get more mud up the bank! Faster, will you?"

Normally the area around Poyang Lake experiences mild weather year round, though icy winds can sweep across the lake during January. Peng's barrack was somehow shielded from those winds, but not the exposed dike a mile away. Cold winds cut through the men's jackets when they mounted the top. To increase labor output, company commanders stationed fatigued laborers atop the dike to record the number of loads each man carried per day. A basket count determined one's food ration, either A, B or C. Since most could only qualify for C ration (half the A ration) some opted to forfeit rations altogether. One could feign sickness, go to bed and live on rice gruel administered to the sick twice daily. Before long one tenth of the company was bedridden.

Peng yielded to the temptation for a few days and while resting in the barrack overheard a 60-year old inmate from the north country ask those around him an odd question: "Fellows, ever notice how ferocious the wind gets on top the dam? But dies down around the barrack? Haven't you thought it strange? There's a reason. Those piercing winds are spirits of dead men wandering over the dike. Next time listen to the shrill sound of wind cutting across the top. Cries they are, cries of men bewailing their fallen comrades who worked here years ago. Next time you get to the top, look at it. Imagine how many thousands of men labored here, how many years it took to build that canal, mile after mile with human hands. Where are the men who worked the river bank last year? Where are they, I ask? Somewhere else, with poles and baskets heaving mud up another canal bank. Or else dead. Dead and forgotten. Lost forever. No one knows, no one cares how many bodies lay buried on these wretched banks.

"This is my last year," he continued. "They say my term is nearly up, but I won't make it. I'm ready to cross the River. The demons laugh when we talk about next year. There'll be no next year for me. 'Be patient. We'll have double portions of rice gruel next year,' you say? Not if the commander has his way. He'll bury our bones on the river bank before that."

All hung on his words. He sensed his soon demise and sure enough was gone in two months.

When next on top the dike Peng heard the shrill wind, this time as a lonesome call of departed spirits. He wondered why those countless men went so docilely to their doom. Why didn't they stage a sit down strike? Why no protest against oppression? Of course, they were damned if they did and damned if they didn't. *We are no different.* There they were—two or three hundred men waddling like canal geese up the bank, chanting in unison, "Hey ho! Hey ho! Hey ho!" From afar it must have sounded like the cries of men being driven into hell by the devil himself.

Peng expressed this dike repair scenario in a poem, later confiscated in a house search during the Cultural Revolution. That it drew censure is self evident.

> Over banks of the Poyang, grey clouds hover,
> Wild geese flock to the slopes.
> They cry, "Hey ho! Hey ho! Hey ho!"
> They bear earth on wings bent like arched *biandan*.
> They cry, "Hey ho! Hey ho! Hey ho!"
> Through wind and rain
> Tucking soil morsels under wing,
> Gasping, panting, wild geese

Waddle to the abyss.
Soaked to the skin,
Wrapped in black criminal garb,
Straining under crushing loads,
Their thin legs stagger,
"Hey ho! Hey ho! Hey ho!"
Shrieking at heaven, shaking the earth,
Piercing cold winds snap my *biandan*.
My ears ring, my eyes grow dim,
My strength wanes, my legs crumble.
I pause to bathe at the River Styx.
From hell's abyss to the outer gate,
I see them come. A line from the north,
A line from the south, staggering to their fate.
Groaning, gasping, up from the pit they crawl,
Shoulders swollen, hands gnarled, living skeletons.
Coolies build the river dike, they bear earth,
Earth, earth, as earth bore them.
Cold winds bear their vengeful cries,
Yet find no cracks to enter halls where
Brightly clad women wait on feudal lords
Brandishing swords in wild delight.
Tongues out, bound securely,
Five thousand geese, no fifty thousand, no

Numberless geese clinging to the mud bank
From the abyss they come, to the abyss they go.

32

A first-time viewer could mistake Poyang Lake for a vast ocean. Yet, when one thinks of the open sea, deep blue rolling swells come to mind. What Peng was seeing from atop the canal bank, however, was an eerie expanse of motionless grey water. In the distance faint light broke through the clouds, enabling him to distinguish overcast sky from the lake's horizon. He gazed at the foamless sea for some time until the thatched roof of a floating house came into view. It gave him a start. Nearly one-thousand inmates were precariously perched on top of a 15 foot-wide dike. Water was on both sides of the dike; to the right a turgid, gray lake spilling into the dry bed; to the left, a rushing, turbulent river. From where Peng stood there was but five feet to the water's edge and the surface was rising about three inches every hour. At that rate all three battalions would be engulfed in 48 hours.

To make matters worse, it now began to drizzle. Many inmates, despairing of any rescue attempt, kept their eyes riveted on the swollen torrent to their left. Before they realized it, the sun set. Darkness obscured the water level, making them imagine it even closer. Dire predictions passed down the line:

"Looks like the whole battalion will drown."

"What do you mean? Surely they'll send rescue boats!"

"There aren't enough boats to ferry everyone out from the lake basin. They can't rescue 80,000 people."

"I heard that all the peasants upriver fled yesterday."

"You mean we're the only ones left?"

"Why should they worry about getting boats here in time? Abandoning us is only a 1 percent loss. They can live with that."

"Idiot! What are you talking about? That's one-thousand men lost!"

Darkness had brought with it a sense of abandonment. Rain began to pour down, soaking everyone to the skin. With the commander's torch they could see water creeping up the dike from both sides. Here they were, huddled together on top of a thin strand of mud stretched into the murky lake. If their dike went, they'd have to swim one-hundred feet to the other side through that current. Who'd have the strength? But they must. One might make it by heading diagonally downstream. Peng turned to Chen, shouting,

"We must get to the other bank. Let's swim for it!"

Just then, great shouts rose from the men: "Boats are coming! We can see the lights!" The rescue craft were flat barges pulled by tugs, similar to the ones that transported them from Nanchang City. One came alongside Peng's dike. When a horn signaled that all had embarked, the rear vessel became lead tug and towed them in the opposite direction. Each barge carried 300 persons with enough space for each man to lay out blankets and rest. But everyone stood in hushed silence as the flat barge glided over the water. No words could express their relief at being rescued from death. Several broke out their rice balls and munched away.

Peng could not sleep. When he looked over the gunwales at their surroundings, he noticed that the rain had stopped and, by light of the half moon breaking through clouds, saw they had entered a large river, no doubt the Ganjiang. In the still night he could hear faint strokes of the engine. Joy came over him, the joy of being snatched from the jaws of death. Perhaps it was wishful thinking, but a feeling came over him that somehow he and Chen would come through the whole experience alive.

Flood victims attached to communes were normally given token relief in the form of small cash payments and old clothes. When it came to food and shelter, however, they must fend for themselves. This drove peasant victims off to beg in nearby cities. Peng's situation was different. True, inmates had lost their barracks. But authorities were not likely to return criminals home or ask local farmsteads to absorb 1,000 workers on short notice. Temporary quarters had to be found elsewhere. They were, at the Jiangxi Hydroelectric College, empty during summer vacation. There, thanks to the flood, the inmates were to enjoy needed rest. Peng learned from this experience that hardships are in the eye of the beholder. To lake basin inhabitants, the flood came as a disaster; to labor reeducation conscripts, as deliverance from coolie labor.

The Jiangxi Hydroelectric College had been built in 1958. Its dormitories were similar in design to those Peng had enjoyed at the Shanghai Construction Academy. Battalion cooks did better this time. Coached by the college kitchen crew, they kept things sanitary, wore white aprons, and upgraded food quality. Daily, inmates ate a half can of steamed bread at both meals and cabbage soup at one. Many men put on weight, though their actual intake diminished. This was because they did nothing but eat and sleep for one month. Those who had fled the barracks with no clothes on their backs were issued inexpensive blue uniforms.

For the first time in two years the guards treated inmates as human beings. "It's because they're about to release us," quipped someone. The commanders would appear briefly for roll-call each evening and then vanish. Inmates were free to do as they pleased, except leave the premises. Peng noticed a few smiling faces.

At the end of August, company commanders returned in force. Until then, they took turns watching over inmates at night. During the daytime the cats were away. And, of course inmates played, exchanging addresses, humoring one another. Change had come over them: they were more light hearted and felt at liberty to talk with commanders face to face. Finally, one commander, bearing a sheaf of papers wrapped in scroll fashion, entered Peng's quarters.

"Summon the others to come in here. I have something to tell you." Inmate leaders went through the classrooms, rounding up men for a general meeting. The commander continued,

"Thanks to the administrative section of Jiangxi's labor re-education department, you've had a good rest at the college. But classes resume

September 1st. We must leave before then. Floodwater has not yet receded from the Henhu Farm area. Until it does, you will be broken into smaller groups and sent to other farms." After reading off 50 names, including Peng's, he concluded with, "You men leave tomorrow morning. The rest stand by until further notice."

In the commander's absence the men bantered about the significance of the chosen fifty:

"They're the ones with the best physiques. That's why."

"No. It's those with terms ending in March."

"Where will they go?"

"With returnees along, to one of the good farms for sure."

"But they sent returnees to Henhu, didn't they?"

"The situation is different now."

"Cheer up! "We'll be back together again. They're only sending off the fifty until water recedes from Henhu Farm."

"Do you believe everything you hear? He just said that to pacify those of us left behind."

Everyone was talking nonsense. The fifty were especially jubilant; anywhere seemed better than Henhu Farm. Young Chen walked over, looking sad.

His eyes met Peng's as he said, "I guess this is it. Is there any way we can keep in touch?"

"I wonder. They never tell us our destination in advance. I know. Give me your mother's address. I'll write you in care of her."

"Is it likely you'll ever get back to Shanghai?" asked Chen.

"Don't know. Certainly not if I lose hope."

Chen and Peng talked late into the night, munching on biscuits. How hard this parting would be! For two years they had struggled together.

"When my term is up, I'll go to Qinghai Province where mother is doing labor re-education," said Chen. A year later Peng sent a letter off to Qinghai. No answer ever came.

33

After returning to Nagaoka from Shanghai in January 1960, Yuki waited for the expected contracts with *Mitsubishi*. None came, and his letters to Peng went unanswered. Had something happened? He could not forget the camera-flash incident. While in Shanghai Yuki learned about *xia fang*, the "transfer downward" movement that uprooted thousands of urban intellectuals and sent them to the countryside, all designed to strip bourgeois attitudes from suspected reactionaries. *Perhaps they conscripted Peng for labor re-education*, he thought.

From Nagaoka Yuki wrote several Japanese writers whose poems Peng had translated into Chinese. Had they heard from Peng? No. "But your story of the camera flash," one poet wrote, "prompted us to place a notice in the *Journal of the Asia-Africa Authors' Conference*. It read: 'Anyone knowing the whereabouts of Yinhan Peng, please contact *Journal* editors at once.'"

Several months after the *Journal* notice appeared, a memorandum was issued by the Shanghai Central Committee to the effect that all arrested overseas-Chinese were to be re-investigated and all those deserving freedom released. Whereupon, in May 1963, an order for Peng's release came to the Poyang Basin labor re-education farm. Peng booked passage on a river boat back to Shanghai, but when he arrived at the Shanghai Overseas Chinese Affairs office, officials evidenced no knowledge of the directive. He stayed with friends while waiting for bureaucratic red tape to be cut. That would not happen until Peng demonstrated the kind of contrition labor re-education was designed to induce. Peng didn't know this. He studiously avoided higher-echelon cadres at the Construction Academy, though they were waiting for proper salutations from their former employee. After two months of waiting, at the end of July 1963, a compromise was struck. Peng was ordered to perform coolie tasks at the Academy: haul cement bags, mix concrete, and cart it to a construction site on campus.

Through the persistent efforts of friends, however, the *Journal* notice finally caught the attention of Premier Zhou Enlai. In the spring of 1964, a directive came from Beijing to the Academy, ordering the administration to reinstate Peng with full professorial rank. He was 44 at the time.

EPILOGUE

"Please come to see us," announced a Kodansha International staff member over the phone. "In Shanghai I think we have found China's leading scholar of the Japanese language. Peng's his name, a professor at Tongji University. He came to our booksellers' convention. At his home I showed him a copy of your phrasebook. When I asked him if he could give time to translating it into Chinese, he showed interest, especially when he heard you were a missionary. Next month he's coming through Tokyo en route to the U.S. Why don't you meet him here at Kodansha?" That was October 1980.

Three weeks later, aboard a train for Kodansha Publishers in downtown Tokyo, I wondered about Peng's Japanese proficiency. During a week's tour of China in 1979, I had searched in vain for such a scholar. At Japanese language departments in Beijing's Institute of Foreign Languages and Shanghai's Fudan University, I discussed the project with Chinese instructors. I noted that their limitations in Japanese were similar to mine. Would Professor Peng's Japanese be any different?

To my astonishment, I discovered he was a native speaker. During our brief times together, Peng's eyes flashed with excitement as he took in Japan's achievement during his 27-year absence. "Japan has accomplished what Chinese socialism promises, and that in a free society," he exclaimed.

"Why did you return to China in the first place?" I asked.

"In 1953, I was finishing my M.A. in economics at Keio University. Just then, Zhou Enlai appealed to patriotic Chinese living abroad, asking that they return to help reconstruct the new China. I was one of those who responded from Japan. My family in Taiwan, who had sent me to Tokyo for a Japanese education, was not happy with the idea. But to a Chinese patriot, the prospect of helping rebuild China was a call to action. I went for a three-year term, much the same way you Americans do in the Peace Corps."

From Tokyo Peng flew to LA and his sister's home and then came to Newport Beach where we worked on the tri-lingual dictionary all summer.

In the process we discovered I had made a false assumption. Finding English equivalents for Japanese phrases, I could do; finding Chinese equivalents for Japanese, Peng could do. But who could guarantee equivalence between all three languages? No one. But we must try. Hot debates between us became the norm. Often Peng's temper flared. His labor-reeducation experience had taught him assertiveness.

At summer's end the 300-page manuscript was sent to a Hongkong publisher, after which Peng went on to New York to visit another sister, and settled down there. Brooklyn became his base for writing on China's progress toward freedom, in Chinese for Taiwan consumption, in Japanese for literary friends there.

In the summer of 1987, a Chinese-Japanese cultural exchange camp was held at Jilin (formerly Harbin) University in Changchun, orchestrated by a Hongkong-based foundation. Seventeen Japanese Christian students volunteered. With pages from the *Japanese-English-Chinese Handbook of Idiomatic Equivalents* in hand they flew from Tokyo to Beijing and headed northeast by rail. Leaving Beijing Central Station, the Changchun Express picked up speed.

The Japanese students were in high spirits, peering out windows, watching green fields and small villages race by. In the far distance, they saw where the Great Wall ends. At Changchun, a university bus carried them from the station down city streets and through the university gate.

Inside they were ushered to their quarters where they prepared to bed down for the night. Touring the campus next morning they wondered about chips out of concrete walls, pock-marks marring the face of university buildings. "Red Guards sprayed the university with gunfire during the Cultural Revolution," they were told.

From 10:00 in the morning the students drilled their Chinese hosts in the proper use of Japanese phrases. Roles were reversed in the afternoons as their hosts taught them elementary Chinese. In the evenings, Chinese students taught elements of Chinese culture; Japanese students shared their Christian faith.

That same summer in Brooklyn Peng suffered a massive stroke. In September I made my way to King's County Hospital and found Peng in good spirits but unable to walk or speak. As I entered the ward, Peng raised his left hand and with sparkling eyes gave a shout, "Ohhhh!" I noticed tears roll down one cheek. How ironic to see this strong man, whose body and spirit could not be broken by his captors, now in the midst of freedom, confined to a wheelchair. From nearby patients I learned Peng was attending Sunday worship services conducted by the hospital chaplain.

Before leaving I walked behind the wheelchair, placed both hands on his shoulders and prayed for him in the best Japanese I could muster. That same year his wife came from Shanghai to care for him, but the stroke had taken its toll. Peng passed away before he could return to see China adopting economic reforms he had advocated.

In 1973, while walking home from work, Yuki was struck by a motorcycle and died. He was given a Christian funeral in the church where he found faith. Shin and his family live in the old homestead; he serves as a Christian educator in the Nagaoka school system.

In a small condo overlooking the Pacific Ocean, Matt. Jr. writes these words. Rising out of the blue sea, Catalina Island evokes memories of the Japanese archipelago, her people and the experiences that transpired there.

www.ingramcontent.com/pod-product-compliance
Lightning Source LLC
Chambersburg PA
CBHW022131080426
42734CB00006B/317